Wisdom of the Masters

WISDOM OF THE MASTERS

▼

Carol Sydney

Writers Club Press
San Jose New York Lincoln Shanghai

Wisdom of the Masters

All Rights Reserved © 2001 by Carol Sydney

No part of this book may be reproduced or transmitted in any form or by any means, graphic, electronic, or mechanical, including photocopying, recording, taping, or by any information storage retrieval system, without the permission in writing from the publisher.

Writers Club Press
an imprint of iUniverse.com, Inc.

For information address:
iUniverse.com, Inc.
5220 S 16th, Ste. 200
Lincoln, NE 68512
www.iuniverse.com

The names of clients, other channels, and audience members used in this book are fictitious to protect their privacy.

Cover Concept: Carol Sydney
Cover Design: Alan Aufrance

ISBN: 0-595-19597-0

Printed in the United States of America

*To Kathleen
For always being my friend*

There are more things in Heaven and Earth, Horatio, than are dreamed of in your philosophy.

—*William Shakespeare, Hamlet*

Contents

Acknowledgments xi
Introduction xiii
Chapter 1—Lao, A Beginning 1
Chapter 2—Clio 10
Chapter 3—Clio's Wisdom 20
Chapter 4—Broadening Horizons 30
Chapter 5—In Transition with Rocando 38
Chapter 6—Sananda 49
Chapter 7—St. Germain 59
Chapter 8—Archangel Michael 66
Chapter 9—Djwal Khul 73
Chapter 10—El Morya and the Garden of Being 89
Chapter 11—Kuthumi: Friend across Time 99
Chapter 12—The Unifying Power of Self-Love,
        Cellular Healing, Part II 114
Chapter 13—Living in the Magic, Cellular Healing, Part III 124
Chapter 14—Surrender to Love 134
Chapter 15—Mother Mary's Blessing 142
Chapter 16—Finding Purity of Heart 154
Chapter 17—Let Me Be Your Comforter 165

Chapter 18—Kwan Yin and the Open Heart 173
Chapter 19—Moccasin 182
Chapter 20—The New Ghost Dance 193
Chapter 21—The Dance of Peace 201
Chapter 22—What Lies Beyond 209
Appendix A 215
Appendix B 222
About the Author 225

Acknowledgments

There were so many people who helped make this book possible it is difficult to name them all. My clients have taught me more than I had hoped to learn in this lifetime, and I am indebted to each one of you. It is, indeed, an honor to work with you; I thank each one of you for trusting me with your most tender secrets and deepest intimacies. I am humbled by the love and cooperation I receive constantly from the other side, both from my guides, the masters, and from those who have crossed over.

The most special people are those who have been encouraging me from the beginning and holding such a beautiful light for me to stand in and see who I am; this book is your accomplishment also. Thank you to Patia and Gwendolyn for your invaluable assistance and guidance; to Val Ann for encouragement and support; to Candy and Ron for being family; and to Ron for always saying, "How's the book coming along?" Thank you to Karen for being a kindred spirit; to Debra for sharing our secret world of the other side; to Michael for always being an example of non-judgment; to Jo for your kindness, acceptance and play; to Jan for never giving up, to Jane for all the support, encouragement, and unconditional love, and for all those little things too numerous to mention; to my English teachers, endless gratitude, and to all my readers who tell me to keep writing.

Introduction

As I felt the essence of Mother Mary merge with my own consciousness, it was as if I was dissolving into her body and yet it was more than that. We were merging together into oneness. Even though I had not left my body to channel her, I could no longer feel it. I felt as if some great unseen hand was pouring liquid velvet into me. I was no longer who I was as Carol Sydney; I was a combination of both Mary and I together.

The experience was unlike anything I had ever felt. I had not felt this before even in visions with my own beloved master guide Kuthumi. I'd been channeling for years and had never felt so complete. I finally understood what it meant to be loved by God and even as I was feeling and thinking these things, Mary spoke to my mind saying, "You are loved even a thousand times more than this my child." It was so much more than I could ever have asked or hoped for.

I continued on with the session while my client on the other end of the phone was still listening to what Mary was telling her. I began describing the sensations I was having to my client in hopes that she too could join in this oneness, but she could not. However, her distance from the experience did not diminish my own joy at this remarkable joining with Mother Mary. It was such an effortless feeling. I wanted to know more about it and why it was happening to me, so as Mary was talking to my client through me, I spoke to Mary in my mind. In my other experiences with channeling, I had discovered that I could hold a separate conversation in my mind while the session with a client was in progress. I didn't even have to form coherent words or complete sentences; I rather 'felt' my question in a vague emotional way, and the guide who was merged with me could understand.

I asked Mary how this complete joining of our two beings was made possible. She told me it was a combination of factors coming together in divine synchronicity. I had learned how to surrender to Mary weeks before and was curious just how deep the surrender could go. In my willingness and trust to allow her to be with me in this way, she was giving me love I had never before been given in physical form. She told me our work together was just beginning and that it would take me across the country and around the world. She thanked me for being her vessel and told me she had much more to share with me as time went by. I sensed this would all be laid out for me without having to plan exact dates or details. I could relax and know all was well.

I wanted more information, so I sent another thought to her, "How is it I can do this now but was unable to before?"

"It is your surrender, trust, and faith in me that makes this possible," she said. "My skill and ability to cross the veil corresponds with your faith, and we meet halfway. It is neither you nor I that do the work but God itself. Because God is love, when you surrender to me, you also surrender to love. This love you are experiencing is you, too. I already experience being one with God and because of this, I know I am love. You do not yet *know* this, but by joining with me you can feel the love that I am; you can feel that I am one with God. You can now feel you are one with God, too."

I sensed she was telling me something about which I could only grasp a microscopic part. She began teaching me what she meant by the word *know*. I was learning a whole new vocabulary, spirit's vocabulary. Each word had a different meaning, untouched by the fear of our world. By *know*, she meant become one with, take inside of my soul and spirit and merge with, as I was merging with her. She showed me how in her world of love there is no such thing as separation from God or love. You wanted love and it was yours, it was a simple as that. Ask and you shall receive.

A whole new realm was opening for me that I previously only dared glimpse. I was falling in love with Mary and her world. I wanted to be a part of everything that was changing in the Earth, so I could help others feel exactly what I was feeling then: certainty that love is here for us and that it is literally ours for the asking. I knew then that nothing separates us from love but our own fear that we will not receive it when we need it or ask for it.

I concluded the reading with my client on the phone and sat silent for a long time, still reveling in the aftermath of what was to be only a beginning of my new life as a channel. Mother Mary had become so much more to me than just another master. She was now a kindred spirit, a trusted, beloved friend and comrade whom I was certain would be at my side through the rest of my journey here on Earth. As a friend, I intimately felt our equality. A new peace came over me so reassuring, I wondered how I could be afraid of anything ever again.

My life had changed in that hour, and I was never to be the same. But it was not always like that in my channeling. In fact, I started out quite a skeptic about channeling, not ready to believe in any of it. Even though I had been channeling for several years, even though as a child I had always wanted to be a psychic, even though this was now the path I was now on, I still had a long way to go.

* * *

Many people have asked me what it is like to channel. Do I leave my body? Do I remember, or even hear, what is being said? I often say it is like standing in a small closet with the light turned off, waiting for someone to walk in and join me. Because it is a small space (as my body is) I scoot over to one side of my inner being to allow someone else to enter. In sharing this modest space with a guide, or the energy of several guides, one can imagine it is quite intimate. As I stand in this private, inner space, I allow my intellect to feel as if it is floating. I become unattached to what is being said and do not interact with the information as it is spoken. I am sometimes even surprised at what I hear, not knowing what will be said until it is said.

I listen to the guides' words as they are spoken and often feel as if I am standing across a large open space some distance from my body. The feeling of openness is very pleasant, and I always feel relaxed and peaceful. I can also sense the emotions I personally have for the particular guide I am channeling. I am closer to some guides than others. I can also usually feel what the client is feeling. My empathic and other psychic gifts seem strangely unaffected.

My feelings for Mary and Kuthumi are the strongest, as they are my closest friends. Though they do not have physical bodies, when I am with them I feel I am surrounded by loved ones with whom I can joke and play. It's a scintillating experience that fills me up and gives me almost more joy than my relationships with friends here. Though I rarely feel alone, I always feel a sense of privacy with matters of the physical world. Perhaps this is because I know my guides never judge me. Even when they watch me make silly mistakes, I still feel cherished. They are fond of pointing out things to me in such a humorous way, I can't help but laugh at myself. Instead of laughing at my expense, they always laugh with me, and it melts my heart. For the rest of my time here on Earth, I will never have any doubt that I am completely loved.

In channeling the ascended masters and archangels, I do not always sense a difference between them and me. In fact, I experience such a blending of our energies in the channeling process that I often marvel at how I can return to a world where people believe they are actually beings separate from one another. We are all connected at the soul level, and this is what I feel when I am in the higher realms. It is a feeling I miss when I am not there.

The truth of it is I don't consider myself separate from the guides I channel at all. It would be just as easy for me to say "This is the Kuthumi part of me," or "This is the Mary part of me." It feels as accurate. I have read many critics of channeling who say it is only a valid method of teaching if the channel can take responsibility for speaking instead of some being or discarnate master. I believe this comment is not entirely unfounded. Since I am aware of my own spirit joining with the masters as I channel them, I know I am an active part of the teaching, as both a part of process and in the message taught.

In fact, both the message and the energy are important aspects of channeling. The energy and love transmitted into our third dimension is often more profound that what we can receive on an everyday basis, so it is not enough to just listen to the words. Often the level of insight you receive is directly related to how well you are able to engage the energy given with it. Sometimes the mind cannot understand what is happening until there is a willingness to receive the love alongside the words. Once the love is received, the hearts opens, and you understand the vibration as well as its message in words.

One might well ask how it is possible to 'understand' a vibration or energy. The answer is a simple one. In taking in energy without engaging the intellect, much is received on a body and heart level. When you receive a hug from a friend or loved one, you don't try to understand what is happening inside of you. You just receive it and allow yourself to feel good. It's the same with energy from higher dimensions. These energies or messages from other realms have the power to heal, soothe, and comfort just as we are able to do these things for each other here in the physical plane.

Is it really all that important who is speaking to us if we receive love in the process? If the love brings us closer to who or what we are, then listening with an open mind and heart is all that is necessary. The masters are no different than we are. We are their equals. This is always the way they encourage us to see them. Try treating them as you would a long-time friend.

As you read about the masters, remember, I know only how they appear to me. No doubt, they will come to you in a way you are easiest able to receive them. However with each master or angel you meet there will be something unmistakable about them, something unique to them as individuals. Though we are all a part of the oneness, whether in the physical or in spirit, we each retain our individuality and uniqueness.

The individuals you will meet here might well intrigue you. Some of you will find Sananda much the same as he was in body, when he was here as Jesus the man. Some might not be able to see him as one who speaks in everyday language without his words being couched in the metaphors of old. Clio may appear to some to be a strange blend of human and animal. Are the lines drawn between the animal kingdom and humans really so distinct, or do we all drink from the same pool of life, which graces us with its bounty and allows us all to share equally in this wondrous place we call Earth?

Some of the beings in these chapters have been with me since my childhood and some for many lifetimes. Others are new to me, or so they seem, though because my perspective is sometimes limited to the scope of this dimension alone, I often wonder if I know far less than I think I do. Undoubtedly, this must be true.

Perhaps when you have felt the energy of Michael wanting to help you so much that it seems to almost hurt him, you too will feel a certain kinship with him. Though they are etheric, these buddies of mine in the heavens have so many ties to our little planet that the boundaries of who they are and who you are can become blurred. This can allow you to feel a oneness of spirit with them, making the differences between you not just intangible, but meaningless.

"Imagine a God", they say, "whose lap you can sit on and talk for hours about the little things." Sound a little like Santa Claus? Maybe the analogy isn't far off. I've often thought of the Santa depicted in the movie *The Miracle on Thirty-Forth Street* is a little like the kind of God I believe in. Oh, my God isn't human, of course, or even male, but if God is as kind, funny, and loving as that old Saint Nick in the movie, then I think my journey as a human holds lots of fun and joy. If the journey doesn't include laughter, then I want no part of it.

Getting to know wise spiritual beings as my own personal teachers is an awesome thing. Coming to know them as intimate friends, buddies in the world of spirit, is pure bliss. It is also intriguing, humorous, perplexing, sometimes frustrating, and always unpredictable. Perhaps it the ever-present surprise that keeps me coming back for more. I always like to be entertained and my friends in spirit do that quite well.

As you meet my friends one by one in these chapters, you will see they are individuals in the truest sense of the word. Always unique, these beings of light are my guides and companions not only in the upper worlds of energy and formlessness but in the everyday decisions and problems I have had to make here in my life on Earth. Whether they are guiding me in making career decisions or helping me through choosing which socks to wear on any given day, they have always been helpful, kind, and loving.

Welcome to the fascinating and loving world of the ascended masters. It has become my home away from home and a place where I now greet some of the best friends I have ever had, the masters in this book. As you read, let the words flow over you. Let the understanding come gracefully and not all at once. Working at understanding something is often the mind's way of trying to control what it cannot comprehend. The heart has its own way with things. Its own way of bringing something in and mulling it over until it is at peace with it. Let it be so with these words. Let your heart feel what is written here, let your mind be only the vehicle that brings the words into your heart.

Use the information in this book as a supplement to your own knowledge, not as the final word. In meditation and communication with your own spirit guides and angels, you might find similarities to my experiences, or you might find vast differences. There is no one right way to communicate with those in spirit. Use my description of each being as an aid to help you receive instruction from the guides with whom you resonate with the most. Use it to reassure yourself that the guides and angels are as real and as individual as each one of us. Trust, and you will receive their love and companionship. They will try every way they can to make themselves known to you. It will be up to you to have faith and to be willing to let go and listen.

In connecting with your own guides, the words "Ask and you shall receive," were never more truly spoken. Receive well, and enjoy the feelings of love that come with every answer, every bit of assistance, and every bit of guidance. These friends of mine want so much to meet you and let you know that you have all the help in the universe at your disposal. Call upon them often; they stand ready to serve you. It is why they are here. One more thing: Don't forget to laugh with them as they chuckle at the foibles of our humanness, which they find so entertaining. You might just end up laughing at yourself. Just when you are being too serious, they will often send you into humorous situations, designed to laugh you right out of your stress and fear.

Take these energies in and allow them to give you new insights, new awareness of your unity with other people, and a renewed sense of hope for a peaceful way of living on Earth—a planet that seems to be getting ever-smaller by the day. Remember the dreams you once had about how we could all live together in peace. It all starts with you, and remember, peace is an inside job.

For those of you new to channeling or to New Age ideas, it might be helpful to define a few terms or at least give a basic description of the different dimensions and etheric realms. I have also included, as Appendix A, a list of the guides channeled in this book with a description of attributes and characteristics you might find useful to identify and communicate with them. In Appendix B is a sample meditation, which might help those not experienced with formal meditation practices. As a note of interest, I have rarely practiced any formal mediation myself, but rely instead on quiet moments during the day to find the peace I require.

As we evolve, we are increasingly able to experience the full range of love and energy in the higher dimensions. We begin with our own third dimension, the physical world. It is a world of duality, where for each feeling of happiness there is a corresponding feeling of sadness to balance things out. In truth, happiness and sadness are but two sides of the same coin.

To understand the fourth dimension, it is helpful to know it exists alongside our third dimension and is a place of transition we visit between life times. It is a world of God's grace, where love flourishes and where there are specific rules about loving one another. It is not as much a world of free choice as we experience here, but a world where we learn how interconnected we are and how our actions affect others. In this safe place, we live together, learning from one another, in the free-flow love in preparation for another life in third dimension.

The fifth dimension is a world of light that never darkens. It is a reality that never doubts, never judges, never fears, and never stops loving. When we are in direct contact with the fifth dimension, we too feel the love, joy, and freedom from fear that is endemic to that realm.

The Fifth dimension is like the sky in a way. It surrounds us here on the Earth but is not exactly a part of Earth. It gives us beauty and light, often inspiration and peace, but it is hard to hold onto. It is the etheric, the fleeting, the ephemeral world of spirit that guides us, reassures us, and loves us not from a distance but from right inside our own hearts. It penetrates our world and us as well. That is the nature of love, always seeking to incorporate more into itself. For those of us who are able to surrender long enough to make contact with it, it is our new destination as the human race. It is not only where we are going as a planet and as a species, it is something that lies already in our hearts and souls. It is home.

There are other dimensions beyond the fifth and though I do not consider it relevant to identify each one here suffice it to say that the higher you go, the more love, peace, and joy awaits you. Many of the masters exist in realms far beyond ours. They teach us from a place we cannot comprehend nor ascend to yet, though the dimensions beyond the fifth are our destination, too. The fifth dimension is simply a jumping off place, where we can come together and regroup in love before moving further on into greater oneness.

Just because the guides and masters mentioned in this book inhabit these realms of light and harmony does not mean they are higher or "better" than we are. In fact, they constantly remind me, and those to whom they speak through me, that we are the same. They hold the plan for Earth in their spirits, and they are your guides as well as mine. They are here to assist us all in coming to remember that we are wise and wonderful beings of light. If you will simply call upon them, they will leap to your aid and be glad to do it. All you have to do is open your heart and be willing to listen. Though willingness will not get you all the way there, it will ensure that you connect. Then, if you remain open and willing, you will be guided to take actions that move you in the direction of union with divine love and harmony. The most important thing they have come to teach about is our own perfection.

On occasion, I have had the privilege to make connection with those loved ones who have crossed over into the realm of spirit to continue their journey. On one such occasion, a young woman named Karen came to me. She had just lost a close friend to suicide, and she wanted to see if I could contact her. A bit humbled by the request, I said I would try. After only a brief moment, her friend approached me from the other side to tell Karen the following:

"Hello, Karen, I've been wanting to talk to you so much! I'm fine, and I feel so much love here all around me. Please don't worry about me, instead, take care of yourself. You have no idea how much love is around you all the time. It's in the trees; it's in the flowers. The very air you breathe is full of love! It's what you are all made of. It's in the faces of those you see on the street, even when you don't know they love you, still they do. I couldn't see this when I was 'alive' but now I know how much I was loved, even then."

I realize in being a psychic and channel, I hold a rare and powerful position that I don't take lightly or without the utmost respect toward those who ask me for guidance and place their trust in me. My clients often honor me with such kind words of thanks and gratitude that it fills my heart to overflowing. I never cease to marvel at my clients' devotion to the truth and their courage, gentleness, and strength in the face of adversity. I am grateful to them and feel privileged to be a part of their path. I could never return the kindness they have shown me, it is so great. In truth, I have to say, the honor is all mine.

Chapter 1

Lao, A Beginning

It's difficult to say exactly when my career as a psychic began. Psychic since birth, I would often share bits of information with my family that I had no way of knowing through education or life experience. Once, when I was in second grade, my mother and older brother were having a history discussion for a paper he was writing for a fifth-grade assignment. They were trying to remember the name of the Indian guide who led Lewis and Clark through the northwest frontier. With consternation, furrowing their brows, they concentrated on the question to no avail. I listened to them as I sat playing with my jacks nearby. I quickly grew irritated and said in my seven-year-old profoundly disgusted voice, "Oh, you know, it's Sacajawea," pronouncing perfectly a name I had never before heard spoken. They stared at me open-mouthed as I said her name with ease. I was amazed at how silly they were. Didn't *everyone* know that?

Though my career as a psychic was not to begin in earnest until years later, as a teenager I read all the books about Jeanne Dixon I could get my hands on. Ruth Montgomery was a favorite of mine too, and I plowed through her books as well. I learned all about spirit guides, automatic writing, and communicating with the "other side." I remember trying automatic writing and even what was then called *stream of consciousness* writing. All I can remember producing from those first attempts was the phrase, "Look past the wall, the wall behind your mind." For a kid in junior high school, it was not a bad start.

After such an auspicious beginning, my next step was to send away for pamphlets on the Rosicrucians. I continually had to ask for help in understanding what I was reading, but I forged ahead nonetheless. I remember coming across the word "oneness" in my mail-order literature and was intrigued when my mother told me it meant being together with God. I was hooked and wanted more. I received a gift from my mother at Christmas time, a Ouija Board, which was put into immediate use. I studied all the "occult" material, as it was called then, I could get my hands on and still hungered for more. I read in a book about Jeanne Dixon that she had a star formation in the palm of one of her hands that foretold her life as a psychic. I held seances with my friends and stared endlessly at my own palms, hoping for a similar sign.

The high school I attended was a converted army hospital from World War II, and I remember taking my Ouija Board there after school hours. During football games on Friday nights, my friends and I would sneak into the older part of the school, hoping to contact the spirits of people that had died there. On one such night, the Ouija Board moved with peculiar speed, spelling out a message so vivid, and none too happy, we all packed up and went home, leaving the dark and crumbling walls to listen to the messages.

As I grew into my teens, new priorities began to take precedence over my intuitive abilities; things like boys, dancing, rock & roll, and especially the Beatles became ever more exciting than spiritualism. My parents were busy with their lives, too, and I was often left to my own plans of sleepovers and after-school activities. It wasn't until much later that I took up my native abilities once again and went in search of the mysterious. I wasn't to be disappointed.

My earliest experiences with channeling began when I attended channeling sessions held by others in the early '90s. Shortly after college, I moved to Montana to find my truth in the Rocky Mountains. My first such encounter came shortly after I started dating a young man in my adopted hometown of Kalispell. He came over to my place one Saturday afternoon and suddenly announced he had just been to a channeling group where discarnate entities spoke through a woman to a small audience. Listening to him describe his afternoon experiences, I was charged with an energy I had never felt before. It was as if I was being lifted right out of my chair! I knew in that moment that nothing that happened next in my life was as important as finding a way to attend the next channeling session. The very next Saturday I had my chance.

My friend and I arrived a little before noon at a local business in town. The channeling session was being held in a small back room of a New Age bookstore. Even though by the early 1990s there had already been many books expanding upon what used to be seen as the occult, small-town living in Montana was still quite conservative. It didn't matter to me if other people in town thought I was strange or on the fringe, nothing could have kept me from the event that day.

When we arrived there were already a number of people seated in the audience, which consisted of about a dozen men and women of varied ages. Some, like me, had never attended a channeling session before, and I could see they were as eager as I was. The people were seated in metal folding chairs placed in small, neat rows facing one over-stuffed chair to be occupied by *Monica*, the woman who would channel. They spoke in hushed voices as we all waited for things to begin.

I had no idea what to expect and though my friend told me all that had transpired the week before, I was mystified and intrigued—ready for anything. My powerful curiosity, fed on early years of desire for "other worldly" experience, made me open to receive and eager to experience spiritual phenomenon.

When the audience was seated and quiet, Monica entered the room. She was a woman in her forties and by her diminutive size and quiet demeanor, I couldn't see how anything too powerful could come through her. She removed her shoes and sat crossed-legged before the audience in the chair in front of us. She was dressed casually in slacks and a white cotton blouse. She had a calm and pleasant air about her while she chatted quietly with members of the audience before the session got going. I was struck by the simplicity of the scene. I don't know what I had imagined, an incense-filled room, perhaps, with Eastern music in the background? It was nothing of the sort. A very simple, even innocuous picture filled my view, and I immediately relaxed into my surroundings. I hadn't even known I was feeling nervous until then.

Monica began by giving a short explanation of what channeling is and told us all to relax. She said we would feel a change in the energy in the room and would probably enjoy the feeling. She said she would be channeling Lao, a two-thousand-year-old Tibetan monk. She closed her eyes, relaxed into the chair, and we waited. It seemed only a few moments before the air around her shifted, becoming charged with an almost electric excitement. Her entire appearance changed, her features gently taking on a more Asian look. Her eyes even began to appear slanted and as her mouth turned up into an inscrutable smile, it was Lao who spoke:

"Good afternoon, I am Lao," he said. "I am here to speak with you and answer whatever questions you have. Who will be the first to speak?" His voice and phrasing were a bit stilted, and it took me a moment to adjust to his presence and personality.

As the first of many questions was offered to Lao, I tried to get a feeling of what exactly was happening here. It was obvious to me that it was not the small woman in front of us speaking. It wasn't just her change in appearance that led me to this conclusion, but the feeling of heightened energy that filled the room. It was as if, with every breath I took, I too was now filled with the same electric charge absent before Lao came in. The energy all around me was also somehow different, and I could see others in the room were affected by it, too.

As the group continued and more questions were asked of Lao, something else also became apparent to me—something startling. As some of the audience's personal questions were offered, I found myself "hearing" the answers moments before Lao spoke to the group. What was even more surprising to me was my own casual acceptance of all of this. Not only did I know the answers, I knew that I knew! I also had a strange feeling that made the hair on the back of my neck stand up, an *I-have-done-this-before* type of feeling. I couldn't understand how this could be true. This was my first such session—at least it was in this lifetime.

I had such a strong belief in the afterlife and in other esoteric aspects of metaphysics, I would have been happy to de-bunk any charlatans I found. Ready for anything, I came armed with my highest sense of discernment only to find myself immersed in feelings of calm familiarity I had only felt in my earliest childhood experiences and readings of psychic phenomenon. I was already on the road to being a channel myself. A part of me was not jumping for joy at the realization, but calmly accepting it and waiting for the rest of me to catch up.

The group with Lao was not the only group I attended before I began channeling myself. Though I did attend several group sessions with Lao, I also looked around for more events and groups in which to take part. Many months later, I was invited to a group where an older man channeled a Native American spirit guide. In this group, the channeled being, I'll call him *Macan*, did not take questions from the audience, but spoke directly to each person, offering them information pertinent to their particular circumstance in life. Macan would go around the circle of people in the audience and tell each of them something vital to aid them in moving forward on their spiritual path.

When it came time for him to speak to me, he addressed me with a well-known air, calling me his "old friend." Even though this was the first time I had spoken with Macan, I also felt an instant recognition, something I'd felt as soon as he appeared that afternoon. Again as feelings of calmness sweep through me, I found myself completely at ease while casually talking to a friend from long ago. Though channeling was still new to me, I again had feelings of familiarity and peace, as if I had done this many times before. I began to suspect that these experiences were happening to me for a reason. I had not yet seriously begun to consider becoming a channel myself and yet the more I happened on these encounters, the more I felt myself drawn to exploring my own connection to the world of the other side.

After the group with Macan, the channel sought me out. He told me he was surprised that Macan had recognized me. In his many years of channeling him, Macan had only done that to one other individual, a young man. He went on to say this particular young man had attended only one session. He expressed his desire to see me attend more of the sessions myself and in leaving me commented on how ironic it would be if I, too, attended only the one session. Strangely enough, even though I had every intention of going to more such sessions with Macan, that one afternoon group proved to be the only one I ever attended.

Though I did not go back to see Macan again, I did attend several sessions with Lao. Each one brought new meaning and gradually began to awaken a part of me that had been slumbering for a long time. Soon, I was even to have my own intimate rendezvous with Lao in the most unlikely of places. I continued to seek out other channeling sessions and gradually began becoming involved with other spiritual people in the Kalispell area.

My continued connection with Lao manifested in an interesting and helpful way. One night while on my way to work, I started feeling sadness about my life and the lack of a clear career path. I'd been working in the field of mental health, in a stress-filled private hospital that emphasized quality paperwork rather than compassionate care. I had just about convinced myself that my life would never change, that I was doomed to be a paper pusher instead of the "savior" for people in distress I'd planned on being. I felt that if I didn't get some encouragement about my future, I couldn't go to work one more night. It was in this depressed state that I pulled over to the side of the road before going on to the hospital. I was already late for work, but I knew I needed some help to even get me there. I sat back in the seat of my little truck and asked for some guidance. I knew I needed to find a ray of hope.

As I sat there almost shaking with the thought of an ever-lengthening line of unfulfilling shifts stretching in front of me, a strange sensation started to fill my vehicle. I relaxed into it, welcoming a growing feeling of peace that came to me. I sensed a gentle energy coming nearer to me, and I gratefully accepted the calmness it offered. My body was slowly filled with something I can only call a *presence*, and I was lifted up into a feeling of certainty that all would be well. As I accepted the presence into my own body, my eyes began to take on that certain inscrutable slant. All at once, I knew Lao was with me! He spoke only two words to me, but they were words that filled me with such peace, I could not for a minute doubt their accuracy. "Just trust," he said, and as quickly as he had appeared, he was gone. Knowing I had to hurry to get to work, I glanced at the clock, certain that my experience had put me at least a another half-hour behind. I was shocked to see only five minutes had passed. It seemed like an eternity!

It is almost impossible to describe in words what I felt that night. With just two simple words, Lao gave me all the reassurance I needed. Though he was with me for such a short time, I sensed he was telling me to be calm and not to worry; my prayers for a fulfilling life were being heard. I had guides of my own who, in time, would come to me and show me all I needed to know. I also knew in that moment there was a purpose in my being at my present job that I could not understand but would become clear to me if I could just wait a little longer and have faith. I felt so certain of all these things, I completely trusted that all was well. I could not have done otherwise, I was again immersed in the feeling of *knowing* everything would be fine and that I was in my right place in the universe.

The experience I had that night in my truck with Lao is the same as my experience with channeling now. When I channel, I share such a powerful intimacy with the beings I enjoy, I can see everything they see and from their point of view. It is impossible for me, from that perspective, to doubt what is being said. I know that I know.

Channeling for me is such pure joy. I am always filled with the same peace I felt that night in my truck with Lao. When I share my body with powerful beings of light, it is a little like being all wrapped up in a soft comforter, snuggling before a fire. As the peace fills me up, I am told to simply begin. I relax and become aware of my own internal space, where my body is, and how it feels. If I feel any anxiety or stress about things in my own life, I breathe deeply and allow my focus to change from my own thoughts and feelings to a more eternal sense of things. In short, I let go. Letting go of anything that might detract from a session with a client or a group allows me to surrender to the guidance I receive from the masters.

Once I have relaxed deeply, which for me now takes only a few seconds, I open myself to whatever experience I might receive from around me. Since the world of spirit is right here with us, I don't like to use words like "above" or "beyond," simply because they suggest a separation which I don't experience. After I've relaxed a guide or master will usually show up with information for me to pass along or ask to be channeled. I am usually so filled with love and peace, it is always hard to come back to the physical world.

Channeling is a little like being in a warm swimming pool except that I feel as if I become part of the water. My boundaries expand to reveal my own spirit to me as well as that of the master being channeled. Our spirits are much larger than the size of our bodies would suggest. Our spirits can fill an entire room and beyond. As I become aware of being quite bigger than I thought, I am also aware that I am not alone in this expanded space.

I am aware that my body is speaking words, but know it is not my mind that is formulating what is spoken. Because of this, I don't always remember what was said. It is an exhilarating and uplifting experience. I have never once had a scary or bad experience when channeling. I am always aware of being loved beyond anything I have ever experienced here on the Earth. Each time I channel, I feel more love than the time before.

Soon after my experience of merging with Lao, circumstances presented themselves that allowed me to leave my job at the mental hospital. It was a huge relief, to say the least. After that, I went on to have a number of different jobs, mostly waiting tables in various restaurants in the Kalispell area. It was a big improvement, one that allowed me to meet many different people, both from town and tourists from other areas of the country. I found I still loved working with people, but without the pressure of a clinical setting, I let go of lots of pressure and stress. It also left lots of time for me to pursue my other interests in the world of spirit.

Chapter 2

Clio

I didn't start channeling right after meeting Lao. Instead, I continued to seek out other spiritual people in the area with whom I could share my experiences and find validation. I was still very green and unversed in the current milieu of New Age thought and sometimes felt at a loss when around those who I thought were more informed spiritual folk. I attended a series of meditation classes and other channeling groups in the area and saw there was quite a range of different styles and techniques. I began experiencing many different things, sometimes while alone in mediation or in groups.

As I met other channels, I saw there were some who enjoyed channeling so much, they thought they were better than other people in some way. It was my first taste of ego-centered channels. Once when attending a channeling session in town, I became so irritated with the channel that I left, never to attend that particular group again. I learned a valuable lesson that night. I saw how ego could interfere with the message being given and how it affected the audience. I wanted no part of it. I vowed that night to devote myself to never being overly proud of what I do, but to focus on the message being given instead of on the part I played in delivering it. I remain grateful to the channel from whom I learned this lesson, who for obvious reasons shall remain nameless.

After attending numerous channeling and meditation sessions, my doubts about the authenticity of channeling gradually diminished. I was faced with an ever-increasing body of information and experiences, both inner and outer, which made remaining skeptical rather pointless. I did continue to doubt what was really happening, though, well into my own work as a channel. I realized only later it was, in part, my own upbringing that made me doubt channeling and even doubt myself for participating in it. As all these doubts and fears of not being accepted for who I am lessened, I fell into step with the most fulfilling job I had ever had.

As time passed an interest in channeling developed on the part of some dedicated spiritual people in and around my area. I naturally gravitated to the groups in which I felt comfortable and avoided the others. It wasn't that the people I chose not to connect with were off base or untrue to whom they channeled. Far from it. Sometimes I felt a group too advanced for me, and I preferred to stay in my comfort zone, learning at my own pace. It was this process of taking things one step at a time that helped me progress at my own rate. I would have to say that patience was the most helpful tool I had. Patience and faith were sometimes all I had when I began to make a shift from having an income paid by someone else to earning my own living as a psychic and channel. In the early years, it was not an easy transition.

I eventually tired of waiting tables. With my own spiritual base of connection and power growing, I took the leap and quit my last job. I rented a small office in a building downtown and hung out my shingle. Business was slow at first, but I was just happy to finally being doing what I had come here to do. It was a feeling of such freedom and relief to finally be able to be myself and let the world know about it. I think many psychics and healers go through similar feelings of anxiety about letting it be known that they are outside of what is still considered common or normal. I often work with new healers, psychics and aspiring spiritual teachers. They have my utmost respect. It is not a path easily chosen nor is it one for the faint of heart.

In beginning to work channeling for an audience, I began by channeling an entity named Clio. Clio was short for a longer name that was, by all my efforts, unpronounceable. Some of the sounds were not unlike the sonar of the dolphins hence unmanageable for the human tongue. Clio was, by her own admission, a dolphin-like being. Always playful, simple and self-effacing, Clio was a clever spirit who revealed about herself only what she wanted others to know. I suspected she was of far greater wisdom and importance than she ever let on.

She first made herself known to me one day in early 1992. I was on the telephone with my friend Nancy, a fellow spiritual seeker, and we were talking about our plans for the weekend. All of a sudden, I was filled with a presence that caused me to remark with sudden surprise and delight, "Nancy, someone is with me. She's a bright entity, and I feel like I can see through dolphin eyes!" This was indeed a new experience for me. My joining with Clio was much different than my experiences with Lao.

She was light and bubbly, so I could discern much more about her than I could with Lao. It was almost as if I was channeling part of my higher self. The merging of our two beings was so complete. It wasn't as if I was lost in the connection either. I could feel my own consciousness, personality and ego, yet here was another that seemed to be a part of me as well. This was the first of my lessons in oneness and in the understanding that though we are all beings of individuality, we share an existence as part of a large collective consciousness I call the oneness of love.

During the week prior to my meeting Clio, I had been practicing opening myself to channel and asking for guidance on a continuous basis. I suppose it would be more accurate to say that I was looking at my watch every ten minutes to see if my pleadings were being answered. With patience not always being one of my greatest assets, I was certain my spirit guides were getting sick of my insistence that the connection happen yesterday. In spite of my incessant demands that they ready me to channel, Clio started making regular visits to me, and I was graced by a presence that was gentle, playful and loving. My joining with Clio was one of a series of events that would change my path forever. She was the first being I channeled on a regular basis, and as our connection and friendship grew, I was once again immersed in my childhood world of magic, oneness and God. I had found my niche.

On that evening in 1992 while talking to Nancy on the phone, Clio was with me, within me, in such a way that I was able to see the world through her own unique perspective. Not vicariously by hearing her thoughts and feeling her emotions, but directly by seeing it though her very essence. I felt then as I do now; it is a high honor to be chosen to do this work. I made a choice to be open to other beings who have teachings and love to offer us here in the third-dimensional world.

That night my attitude about certain things I held to be true was suddenly transformed. Through Clio's eyes, I saw the Earth not as a jumble of varied continents and disparate cultures, but a uniform body of light. Its existence and purpose is to offer oneness to *all* life on its surface and within its waters. This oneness or "one being" aspect was something that puzzled me, and so I asked her about it. It seemed all I had to do was feel a question begin to form within my mind, and she would jump at the chance to respond even before I could finish formulating the question into words, certainly before I could ask the question verbally.

She responded to me silently within my mind with a flow of love that brought tears to my eyes. Her thoughts were not exactly in words, but in an energy that carried complete understanding nonetheless. I will try to capture the essence of her thoughts. "Child," she said, "though you knew things only through your one perspective before, now you have two. Yours and mine. They are not separate, as you believe. In the loving eternity of all souls, we are one. In this way, so is the rest of humankind also one being. In a way, it is also true for the animals and other beings with you.

Everything is a part of the life force here on Earth. In this connection there is light for all. There is understanding of the purpose for which you came to Earth; there is belonging and there is love. I am with you now to give you another way of looking at life, which you will eventually share with all the world."

I was filled with excitement! I felt a joy I was sure must have radiated through the telephone lines to my friend. Back then, I had no way of knowing I would be reaching out to so many across this continent, and beyond. In the loving thoughts Clio gifted me with that evening, I felt a simple peace. If others could feel this peace there would be a lot fewer conflicts. All people would realize there is enough love to go around for everyone.

During that conversation with Clio, I also gained a unique perspective on part of the purpose dolphins have here on this planet and the responsibility they carry. Clio showed me a picture of the globe and superimposed over the surface was a pattern of blue-white lines in a grid I was later to learn was the pattern of Ley lines that criss-cross the Earth. Ley lines are energy structures, flows in the spirit realm that energize and maintain the physical structure of the Earth. They act much the same as the veins in the human body. Our veins carry blood, oxygen, nutrients, and regulate temperature. In the grid system of the Earth the Ley lines carry light, information, and energy to needed places on the Earth's surface. The Ley lines also carry away toxins in the form of lower energy from places that have been damaged or polluted.

Clio showed me how the dolphins repair and maintain the Ley lines on the surfaces of the Earth covered by water that are inaccessible to us and other land animals. When we, as humans, interact with Earth, often in the gratitude we feel for her beauty and the life she affords us, we also send energy along these pathways of light. We all contribute to this process, and we all reap the rewards of it. The dolphins are *essential* to the upkeep of the Ley lines covered by ocean. The grid in these watery areas sends energy deep within the oceans to maintain the planet in places no human could reach.

Again in my mind, I asked Clio about some of the places where the oceans had been damaged by oil spills and other forms of pollution. I have long felt a sense grief for areas like Alaska, which had been the site of these accidents, and for the animals who died or lost their habitats. Pictures of tar-soaked sea birds were forever burned into my mind, along with feelings of utter despair and hopelessness for the recovery of areas such as these.

Clio responded to me with the same sense of love I felt from her before, but now there was a sense of compassion for my struggling with these feelings of loss. She showed me her own feelings about Alaska and other areas on Earth that had been polluted. I was amazed at how different they were from my own! Her feelings were those of light and even laughter! She cautioned me to "clean-up" my own habitat first. I was greatly confused and couldn't understand what she was trying to show me, so I asked her to formulate some coherent thought patterns to illuminate my all-too-slow human understanding.

She began describing in her flowing way how when we, as humans feel fear about a part of the Earth being damaged we actually *send* that fear to the affected area, in this case Alaska. She said the dolphins and whales involved in the re-energizing of the Ley lines for that area were having a difficult time getting past all the fear being generated and sent in that direction.

"Fear," she said, "is what makes our job harder. When you send fear, you also send the vibrations of hopelessness you feel along with it. It is like sending constant telegrams our way, saying how you believe the repair work will never be possible. This is not true of course, for anything is possible, but it is true enough if you believe it is. So please," she continued, "send us love instead. That will help the clean-up work, and it will also help you to feel better about the situation." She seemed much more concerned about me and my fear than she did for the land and waters around Alaska. My limited intelligence was only beginning to grasp the great plan for Earth, and I felt relieved but still very much in the dark.

This is what Clio had meant about doing my own "clean-up" work first. It was an entirely new idea to me to love what was going on instead of feeling fear about it, but it made sense. It was the first of many lessons I was to learn about being responsible for my own inner world before I moved out to touch the outer one. What we feel within is also what we send out to others and the world at large. All that we feel, whether it is love or fear, has an effect. It was now up to me to start the internal clean-up work of my own habitat, my own inner world.

There were times when Clio spoke to others through me about the state of Earth. Often, because of her intimate connection with the animal world, she was asked about how the animals communicated, about conditions in different environments, and so on. What always interested me was how she talked about Earth as a sentient being capable of communicating with us if we would only listen. She showed me how Earth is not a victim of misuse, pollution or damage. "Earth is not a victim at all," she remarked one day. "She is a beautiful being capable of defending herself against any incursions."

"Why then," I asked, "Does she allow so much to go on that *appears* to do harm to forests, deserts, and other ecosystems?"

"Because of her great love for all who live upon her," Clio replied. "Earth does not judge the actions of her people, only you do that. She understands that they all learn through what they do. They are learning through being in their *own* environments, both internal and external, in the world." She will allow you to go only so far and no farther. She will not exhaust herself simply to allow you to learn your lessons. Rejoice in her great bounty, and she responds with love and gratitude for your presence upon her. Earth has untapped resources you have not yet seen or even imagined. Cooperate with her, and she will show you more. Be in union with her, and you will find peace. Above all, *never* underestimate the ability of Earth to heal herself."

I have to say, I didn't fully comprehend how all this was possible, but hearing Clio's words and feeling her certainty made me feel a whole lot better. I have always enjoyed a deeply spiritual connection with Earth, and to know she is not a victim of the greed and ignorance of people was very reassuring. I have passed this information on to many through the years of my work, and it has brought peace to others as well. Knowing that no one is truly a helpless victim is both reassuring and thought provoking. It means we are all responsible for what we create—all we create.

In each session that I channeled Clio or connected with her in my own thoughts, I found myself being drawn inexorably more deeply into the world of spirit, and a growing feeling of peace always ensued. Though I no longer channel her as a separate entity, I know for certain she is with me, aiding me on my spiritual journey, and helping me to see Earth in a different light.

There were many times in my early channeling experiences I held sessions with groups and channeled Clio, giving people a chance to address her and ask questions about their personal concerns. I was always impressed with how lovingly she treated all who spoke with her and how the questions asked of her seemed to help not only the person asking but all those in the group. Perhaps what Clio told me in my first connection with her was true: We are not separate as we think we are but connected at a far deeper level than we can imagine. I was also reminded of something I heard Lao speak of in one of his channelings.

Lao said that whenever a group of individuals gets together for the purpose of receiving information from higher sources, beforehand, there is always a meeting of those individuals' higher selves to decide exactly what questions will be asked when the group actually convenes. In this way there is no duplicating of effort on the part of the audience or the entity being channeled. I began to notice this pattern being repeated over and over again both in groups I held and attended. Amazingly, questions seemed to touch everyone in the groups equally and yet no questions were ever repeated.

Often in each session there was a similarity to the questions that were asked, each succeeding query seemed to build on the next so that a deeper understanding of each issue was reached for all. It was as if we were all running a relay race and "tagging" each other when our turn came to come forward. Instead of competition there was a sense of cooperation that seemed to come from beyond us. This must have been the pre-meeting of our higher selves Lao had spoken of. In addition, though questions were often asked that appeared on the surface to be trifling, it played out very differently in the end; everything was always tied up into a neat little package with all the pieces or questions fitting together.

Though in any given group there was usually a blending of people from different backgrounds, beliefs, and growth levels, there was never a sense of judgment or a placing of values on who got there first. We were all there to learn together and help each other understand more about life and about our spiritual paths. Often, a newcomer would ask a question coming from a place of utter simplicity and innocence that would set many experienced group members back on their heels. We were once told by St. Germain, whom you will meet in a later chapter, "Be careful with what you think you know, for it is there that you will realize you know nothing." Always when younger people attended groups, I was moved by how they knew more than their elders did. Wisdom or simplicity, like beauty, is truly in the eye of the beholder.

In my early years as a psychic and channel, I was privileged to work with a number of adolescents. These young adults carried so much wisdom and energy, it amazed me how their innocence kept them from seeing how advanced they actually were. Lack of experience in life and sometimes a lack of validation for their gifts kept these young people from seeing their true potential. I consider it a gift to be able to show someone, young or old, where their abilities lie and how they can use these gifts to their best advantage and to the great benefit of society.

I try to encourage anyone entering this field of work to begin by trusting themselves. Self-trust is the single most powerful tool in gaining a sense of confidence and discernment. For anyone wanting to become a channel or psychic, it is a narrow path that leads one deep into their own personal issues and into a life that is both challenging and rewarding. The self-knowledge gained and the varied experiences—not to mention the sensations felt—are well worth the effort.

Chapter 3

Clio's Wisdom

When I was new to channeling, I often sat with friends or arranged informal, sometimes impromptu, groups or gatherings for which I channeled Clio. The following excerpt is from one such group. Though the information given that day was intense and detailed, there was also an air of lightness and humor. Not unusually, it was something I had come to expect from Clio.

Clio didn't always talk to us about subjects concerning the Earth but seemed to have an abundance of knowledge on just about any topic. This particular discussion seems to be bound together by a teaching about divine oneness.

Clio begins: "My beloved children, it is good to be back with you and so we reach our appointed time and task. I and others wish to answer the questions you have today and will serve to illuminate your minds in any way we can."

The "others" Clio refers to here are beings like herself, in spirit, who are offering their wisdom through her energy and mine. It is a phenomenon that has remained constant in my channeling experience; an entity appears and though individual, has many "friends" with them with whom they consult for the answers, all contributing to the teaching process.

"We wish to answer the questions you have and we know Carol has prepared an agenda for us. Carol wonders if this presents a problem for us— *her* presenting an agenda for *us* to follow. We are equals you know and anyway, I am more closely aligned with Carol than she has yet to realize. And so we would like to address your questions, if you would suggest where to start. David, I believe you have a question."

Clio and all the guides and masters I channel always seem to know who is ready to ask a question and often what the question is.

David, a regular member of many groups of mine speaks up, "I have a question about relationships, soul mates, destiny, and how they are all tied together. How is it possible to hold the intention of meeting your soul mate and still remain in present time? In other words, how can I avoid living in the future?"

Clio responds, "These are matters of some concern for many people besides yourself. There are in fact those who are far along in their spiritual growth who have not conquered their fear of being alone. Your intention does draw your partner to you and you to them, but it is only in the higher-self consciousness that this is accomplished. When you join with your higher self and feel your desire for partnership, the higher self works in conjunction with what is in your soul's highest good. Even though this desire is in linear time, your highest good is still accomplished.

"For more understanding, let us look to Source, or to Divine Oneness. This is where all relationships have their origin, in the Oneness of Source. Truly there is no separation between any beings since all are one. When you meet your soul mate, many of you say, 'I have found my other half.' Does not this seem to belittle who you are in your own completeness? Rather let us suggest you reformulate your statement and say, 'I have found my own reflection in God.' The soul mate does not make you greater or lesser, it merely shows your own divine reflection of who you *already* are in the oneness. This is how the coming together of two people can truly reflect both their own individuality and their own completeness in God. The truest form of partnership is, of course, your union with your own higher self in God.

"Many on Earth are rapidly reaching this point of understanding, but because of the fervent desire many have of meeting partners and the fear of not having them, there is still much confusion. Relax into the understanding we give you, and allow yourselves to realize that you are your own divine partner. In the oneness, this is true, for in being the divine one that you are there is no feeling of loss or of separation. It is just that in linear time you have lost the perspective of seeing that all exists in the divine moment of now.

"The fear you have of being alone forever exists because you do not see all of yourself in this exact moment. Because of this, you experience separation, but this is all in the mind. You live in this moment alone; your thoughts of the future exist in this moment alone. What will *happen* to you in the future and your fears of this exist in your mind. It is the fear upon which you focus, but your view of the future is illusion. You do not need a partner to complete you, and you cannot create this connection for yourself by acting within the stretch of linear time. You can only recognize two things: You are complete now as you are, and peace will come to you when you believe this. All of this happens within the divine moment of now.

"So you see, when you ask about not wanting to live in the future, you are simply feeling your own fear of devaluing yourself in favor of another. To stay in the present moment is to know that your higher self, an aspect of God, will in time give you all you need, and you are capable of doing this. Your physical mate will simply reflect this to you, anyway, upon her arrival. But if the awareness of your own completeness in God is already within you, then you know your soul mate cannot be far away because your reality will always mirror to you what you hold to be true within. Always remember: 'I am my own divine partner.'"

Another question is presented from someone in the group that also concerns relationships, "Is the institution of marriage obsolete?"

Clio answers, "We see there are many paradigms, many ideas of what marriage is and it is different for every individual on the planet! From our point of view, any two individuals almost never agree on one definition of marriage. The question presented is a pertinent one though. Agreed-upon metaphors, such as marriage, can facilitate much growth for individuals within that metaphor, for it provides a safe structure within which to grow. However, if the metaphor, in this case marriage, does not align vibrationally with each individual, taking into account those energetic needs of each person, it becomes limiting and constricting. We would suggest that you become co-creators in each individual relationship saying, 'What form of relationship do we wish to exemplify?'

"An important point to think about is this: What you choose to engage in becomes an example for others to emulate and eventually follow. You are all the masters of this universe and of your physical world, and you should choose wisely the examples you set for others to follow. Remember that you are building the structures of your New World. So choose your metaphors wisely, for this is what you will teach.

"No longer will the structures you choose to engage in, such as marriage, be forms that come to you as pre-set ideas to which you adhere or conform. Institutions, especially ones like marriage that exemplify what relationships are all about, will be most wisely and widely held when they reflect who you are as individuals. So no, marriage is not obsolete when it is co-created by you and your partner as an expression of who you are from within and of you love for one another instead of when it is an ancient archetype to which you rigidly conform. The structure of marriage is intended to serve you, not the other way around. No external arrangement created by someone else can serve you in your divinity."

In listening to Clio's comments on partnership and marriage, I was excited by how she went to the very deepest meaning of the issue. This is something I have seen all the masters do: give the most meaning they can to the question being asked even if, on the surface, the question seems to be light or frivolous. What is one person's frivolity, though, could well be another's sagacity, as I have learned more than once. I have all too often sat in judgment of someone's question, only to be humbled by the wisdom of the response.

After Clio's discussion about relationships, another regular member of the audience, Tiffany, spoke up asking about her abundance. She said, "In dealing with abundance, what is the process, or what are the steps, for manifesting?"

In her usual light way, Clio responds to Tiffany, "So you would like to see how to write out a blank check and create large bank accounts. You are not alone! How curious, there is much limitation in this. There is much fractionated energy, energy that is split off from individuals and lost in fear, in this process of striving for material possessions. You are not separate from the source of your abundance, and this is where your problem lies.

"Let us simply say that with beings who perceive themselves as divine there is no such dichotomy. With beings who perceive themselves as one with the Unlimited Source, abundance is easily manifested. But if you believe yourself to be separated from Source, and if you believe dollars to be the only aspect of your abundance you can control, you are greatly mistaken. Money is not earned; it is received.

"Many of you still run from your fears, thinking you will be abandoned at some point in your lives by God. This is not true! You are loved in an unlimited fashion. You do not yet see how truly viable your connection with your own abundance is. In order to make a solid connection with your own abundance, you must not fail to believe in your own *lovability*! The truth is that Source, or Creator, created you with your own Source inside of you. Most of you have untapped gifts and abilities, creativity, intuitiveness, healing abilities, and other resources within as well as intelligence designed to produce wealth upon wealth in your world.

"Do not many of you wait and hope to be gifted with checks in the mail or with winnings that appear to drop from the sky? This is not the way to live in harmony. To live in harmony, you must first ease yourself into the world. Interact with the world, the world you are so ready to disparage and discard. To fail to interact with the world is to live in fear of being discarded by it. Do not fear you will be rejected by others or by Source. *Engage* the world I say. Take your place among your friends and fellow beings of much light.

"The animals are not afraid of engaging life are they, my precious ones? See how bountifully they are provided for. They do not pay mortgages, drive cars, or stock up cupboards with food. They live free, they play all day long and sing their songs of joy to the world for the abundance it freely gives them. They are grateful for their freedom and do not weigh themselves down with things they have no need for. The wise ones among you will take a lesson from these wise beings. Let them be your teachers, then you will know abundance. Once you have done this, you will be ready to learn lessons in manifesting.

"For instruction in the ability to manifest, connect within yourself to the faucet of the unlimited flow. Find the spigot and turn it on! Allow the flow to begin. Many of you wait for a physical representation of the abundance before turning on the faucet. This is putting the cart before the horse, as you would say. The limitation is needing to have proof of the abundant being that you are before you can begin spending your inheritance! This is backwards, is it not?

"Start spending money like you have it because, indeed, you do. This will start the siphon of your flow—this is what it means to turn on the faucet. When you approach a faucet to obtain water, you do not wait for water to flow from the spigot before you twist it on. In matters of money this is the absurd image you hold in your minds. You approach your bank account and instead of spending what you have in there you wait for more to come to replace what you will spend in the future. Why not spend what you have knowing more will come? Do this in joy of your unlimited provision and find joy. Be careful, do this in fear of your supply not being replenished, and you will drive yourself into debt.

"You will manifest whatever to project into your future with your thoughts and feelings. Remember, in the divine moment of now, all abundance exists. This is universal truth and one of the laws of abundance. If you start the siphon of abundant flow into your checkbook and then fall into disbelief about your own divine abundance and the truth of you being one with Divine Source, you turn off the flow. Your checks are left floating in the water, so to speak! There is much misunderstanding, much confusion, and much darkness about this for many, many beings on the planet who wish to manifest their true abundance. True abundance is abundance of the spirit. All things flow from this point.

"What do I recommend? Stick to knowing you are divine in all aspects, and you will come into alignment with your true being sooner or later and the money will follow. In knowing who you are there is truth, and in truth, joy. When you are able to feel the flow of joy within your body, you will begin to see that all is in alignment to give you exactly what you need at all times. When you are fully present in this awareness, manifesting is simple. It is only when you leave Divine Source out of the fear that you will not be provided for that you run into trouble. Truly there are many past patterns of fear about this for many of you. Relax, face your fears and find release.

"A key of abundance and of manifesting in this way is simple. Reconnect with the experiences and fears you have had in your past, your fear of not having enough love. For most of you money equals love. If you feel worthy of receiving love, your money will flow. It is as simple as that. Heal your hearts for all lack of love, and you will heal your checkbooks!"

Joseph, a man who had attended several groups before, joined in with a question about credit spending saying, "Clio, what about using credit cards and spending the money that you know will come in the future?"

As I readied myself to hear this answer, I sensed Clio smiling inwardly. She replied with a crooked but cute little smile, "My young friend,"—Joseph was actually in his sixties!—"please notice that I address you so, it is your greed and not your awareness of flowing abundance that keeps you in this situation. It is a dilemma is it not? To spend or not to spend? Remember the more toys you have, the more of your attention they take. Now it is not necessarily harmful for you to have toys, but is it distracting. If you will look at what you are running away from, you will indeed have more abundance of heart, of peace and of love for yourself. Do not fear not being loved and you will not need to spend, spend. Spending money on yourself in this way is to prove to yourself and others that you are worthy of receiving. We are not fooled. You deserve so much more than your toys. You deserve unconditional love. Why not receive it today?"

With Clio everything was so simple. I sensed her mood when she spoke the last sentence to Joseph. To her receiving unconditional love was as simple as breathing. I know she knew how hard it was for Joseph to do this and yet in her simple way she showed him how easy it could be for him. This was always her way with people, an understated humility that called out to us to be more like her. I knew she had more to say so I remained quiet, waiting for her to continue. She did not disappoint me.

"This is a question for many of you I see, she went on, " so I will give you more of my wisdom on this. Credit cards though convenient can be so very troublesome, so very troublesome, indeed. It is spending money you do not have that gets you deep into paradox. Think of the animals again my friends, they have no interest in the future, they live in this moment and have no need of credit. They are provided for already. They have all they need in this moment. This is the ultimate wisdom. Stay in this moment and you will be in peace.

"Move yourself away from this moment and you end up in paradox. The paradox of living in the future. When you extend yourself in this way, you take yourself out of linear time and into a no-time space. You do this far beyond your ability to handle it. By doing this, you take yourself out of context. Out of the context where your abundance exists. Your abundance exists in this time, in this place with you. In this place where you are one with all your feelings, your lessons and your joy within linear time. Be willing to be here and be willing to receive. This is simple too. There is such joy in simplicity, don't you think?

"It is true there exists a non-linear time space where all beings are one. You are not ready for this. Do not ask to go to a place where you will be asked to be one with all you contain right now. Could you do this? Face all your fears now in this moment? I do not think so. So be content being in your linear time and receive the old fashioned way—by asking for it and being willing to face your fears of not being provided for. This is what credit cards are all about, is it not? The fear that when you run out of money, you will not be given more? Face fears my children, face your fears and find peace. Then you will know how to play as the animals do, and you will not need your credit cards any more."

When Clio was done, I came back to my own consciousness and rested in my body as everyone else thought about what had been said. I'd never seen Clio slam someone before, and I was almost worried about Joseph. Her response to him seems almost uncharacteristically harsh. I glanced over at Joseph and instead of his being angry as I feared, he had a look of calm acceptance on his face. He was nodding almost absent-mindedly, focused on his inner thoughts. There was a sadness about him I had not noticed before, but there was also a look of hope that I realized now had never been present. I was intrigued by the changes I saw in him.

I asked him after group how he had taken Clio's response to his question. Joseph was a man of some stature both in height and in his standing in the community. He said he was grateful someone finally had the guts to stand up and tell him the truth. Though a man of means, he admitted he had grown tired of what the material world had to offer him but did not know why he continued to buy things that he found empty. He had come to groups to find out if there was another way of living that offered more "meat." He said he didn't know before that night that it was a lack of love that kept him in the empty pursuits of material things. He spoke of this being a new beginning for him, one that might offer a way out of the dead end he felt he was facing. It was almost as if Clio's tone and words opened a place in this man's heart that could not have been opened any other way—her strength matching his. He found respect for her in it.

I was relieved and a bit disappointed in myself. I had feared that Clio's comments had left him offended. Though, I did know enough at this point in my channeling not to sensor Clio's words, so I stayed in trust and allowed her to push on. It was the first, yet not the last time I worried needlessly about one of the master's answers to a client. The masters' wisdom and their love for people always finds a way to get into a crack in the toughest of hearts. No matter how many times I see them do this, I am always amazed at their skill.

Chapter 4

Broadening Horizons

I eventually held many groups with Clio for people in Kalispell and other towns near by. I would pick a date, let people know I would be channeling and show up to enjoy the festivities that always ensued. Before long, however, I was ready to move on and experience new connections with other masters and guides.

While living in Kalispell, I was in involved with a small circle of friends all of whom enjoyed sitting at the feet of the masters as they taught us, laughed with us, and led us deeper into the world of spirit. I have been blessed at many times in my life with friends who were supportive and encouraging in just the way I needed. This period of my life was no different. I had made friends with two women in particular, who I will call Tanya and Beatrice, about the same time I started channeling. They were both familiar with channeling, having attended many sessions with other channels and, in fact, with many of the beings I would come to know on the other side. Their assistance and guidance proved invaluable to me both in identifying beings who would show up and learning to trust myself as I grew into my new abilities and gifts.

Often when a new being showed up to be channeled in a group session, I could sense someone new but could not identify who it was. Tanya and Beatrice, having met many of these beings before through listening to other channels, not only helped me to identify whose energy I was feeling but to feel safe in channeling them. Though I didn't know it at the time, I was on my way to engaging a very powerful connection with the world of the ascended realm. My understanding of the ascended masters is to know that these beings have often led lives here on Earth before coming to know themselves as spiritual teachers. Buddha was such a person, as were Jesus, Mary, and Kuthumi—masters in the world and masters in spirit, one in the same.

I am often asked how I determine whom it is I am connecting with, how I recognize someone on the other side. I usually explain that it is no more difficult for me to recognize someone's energy in spirit than it is for anyone else to recognize a friend they meet on the street. In the world of spirit, I am now more comfortable and fluid than I am in the physical world. It feels like a more natural place for me to be. Though I love my life here on Earth, the intimate connection I share with my guides feels more like home. In the final analysis though, it is the blending of my two worlds that brings me the most fulfillment and joy.

In my early days of practicing channeling, I learned to set parameters, or boundaries, letting those on the other side know I would not honor all requests to channel just anyone. I made it clear to all in the spirit world that to be channeled by me you must be a master. Sometimes, though it was infrequent in the extreme, a discarnate entity not in possession of much wisdom would show up, trying to fool me into thinking he or she was a master worthy of being channeled for the group. I was not often fooled.

On one night, I remember sitting in my rocking chair after group had begun waiting for the masters to come and share their thoughts with us. A being came to my mind and announced himself as a master. His energy was pretty low, and I wondered who the heck this was—certainly not someone I had met before. I asked him who he was, and all he said was, "Oh, I'm a master, I'm a master!" and then he chuckled. It was the laughter that gave him away.

"Go on, on your way," I said to him in my thoughts, "You're not a master; you're just out having a good time." I felt him smile to himself as if to say, "I had you going though, didn't I?" It was a fun encounter, but I have learned that not all spirits have wisdom to offer even if they say they do. I am still careful to set boundaries when I open myself up to receive, but I haven't been bothered by spirits masquerading as teachers for a long time.

Psychics are not immune to the temptations of ego either. Shortly after beginning to channel the masters, I opened an office in a downtown building. My office was on the second floor. In addition to holding groups, I also did private session for individuals. Once after a client came in and we settled into our chairs, I closed my eyes and began to make my connection with the other side. All at once, my chair started swaying side to side and the room shook. If my perception was right, even the building began to sway. Startled, I opened my eyes to see my client experiencing the same sensations. "Now that's a powerful connection!" I thought to myself with pride. A few seconds later someone knocked on my office door and asked if we had felt the earthquake. Humbled, I replied, "Why yes, of course." Humility is such a leveling thing for the ego.

* * *

With Tanya's and Beatrice's help, I gradually began to learn the names and energies of those in the ascended realm. There was Sananda, who was known as Jesus when he lived here on Earth, St. Germain, Archangel Michael, Kwan Yin, Djwal Khul, and a host of others I would come to know as well. I was hesitant at first to trust my own abilities but soon found that the more I trusted my gifts, the more the expanded. Soon I had so many connections on the other side that it was difficult to ever feel like I was alone. Having felt much aloneness as a child I was grateful for the new friends.

In the beginning of my channeling experiences, I was much in awe of the masters I would meet and channel. Though they repeatedly told me of our equality, it was years before I could completely open up to the idea that I could consider myself a master as well. At first, I saw myself only as the vehicle for the wisdom and information to come through. Gradually through years of working with them—or perhaps I should say of their working on me—I have come to know that my higher self's wisdom equals theirs, and I am one of many in the community of the oneness.

After repeated groups and countless private sessions with individual clients, I now have an unshakable peace about my connection with the masters on the other side.

The master I bonded with the most in the beginning was Sananda, or Jesus of old. I was not religious but knowing this being had been a person who had walked the Earth gave me a certain comfort level in channeling him. Sananda was always gentle. In his loving way, he could reassure me no matter how my day had gone, no matter how much fear I was in, no matter how much self-doubt I had. He was my first real friend on the other side.

When I started channeling him, I found he wanted to physically touch others in the group. Though this was not completely comfortable for me— since it was my body that was doing the touching—I agreed on many occasions to comply. I was surprised to find the people being touched often responded to his/my touch with tears. They could feel the same love flow from him that I felt when I channeled him. It was an amazing experience that I grew to truly enjoy. It was what I had always wanted to do: touch people in a way that made them feel love in their hearts. I had never experienced this in my work in mental health. This was no cold sterile environment where paper work was more important than people. This was my world. This was real.

When Sananda approached me in spirit, he often came in a way that was insistent. It was always gentle and loving but in an odd, very persistent manner. It was almost like his love was determined to get through to me—and to others. He was not to be turned away, and I never minded making the connection with him even if it meant getting out of my own shell to go and touch another person. To understand what it was like for me, imagine if you can, a loving lamb, pounding at the door of your heart, asking to be let in. How could anyone say no?

Along with Sananda there was a being early on called Sanadaria, who often claimed my attention as well. Some say she is the eternal soul mate of Sananda, the divine reflection of the feminine in Goddess form. She, too, had a gentleness I found compelling. I first met her during one of my regular groups. When Sanadaria came to me to be channeled, I first became aware of a warm loving energy filling the room and filtering slowly into my consciousness. It was a feminine feeling, as I understand feminine energy to be. It flowed around and into me like a light breeze wraps around you on an early summer day, reassuring me that all was well and that I was in the presence of someone who loved me more than I could imagine.

I could tell immediately that this was something, someone, distinctly different than I am. A different personality. She was warm, loving, gentle and yet, somehow strong and determined. As well as carrying the feeling of a summer's breeze, Sanadaria was also like the bubbling brook that sparkles and shimmers in front of your feet, asking, urging you to come in and join with its flow.

Sanadaria has the goddess energy, but she presents herself more like an unassuming and humble princess, asking and offering to share space—not demanding to, as Archangel Michael does at times. With Sanadaria, it was simply a gift being offered, an introduction to her. I was grateful and willing to receive this loving connection with her. Her energy—not unlike that of Mary's, though younger in a strange, somewhat indefinable and nonlinear way—was eager to show me new levels of insight.

When I met Sanadaria, I was just getting used to the process of inviting others to come into my space and be near me; I would only later become comfortable offering my body to be used as a channel. I was satisfied at the time to simply experience her presence around me without feeling the need to rush headlong into a full channeling experience. It is to my great benefit that by this time in my life I had learned a semblance of patience. In my continuing path of channeling powerful beings of light and energy, it has been essential to acclimate to this experience slowly, giving all my bodies—especially the physical one—time to adjust to the new vibration.

As I began to feel her energy more clearly, I started describing her to the group. "She's telling me she wants to offer a connection with her, if that is to my liking," I said. "She is hoping I can come to know her as a friend; she says she can show me how to integrate 'living amounts of loving light' in order to raise my vibration enough to channel her in my body." Sanadaria continued to give me loving instruction about what was to come for me in the near future. It felt like a merging of our consciousness, and without realizing it, I was allowing a part of her to join with me and a part of me—I was later to learn—to join with her. "It's always a mutual process," she later told me, "always an equal opportunity to learn from both points of view." I couldn't fathom what she was talking about. It seemed an unimaginable thought, as stuck as I was in my limited, judgmental point of view, thinking I had nothing whatsoever to offer *her*, an ascended being from higher planes of existence.

Channeling was beginning to become a learning experience in itself, not just a goal or objective to be achieved. To become a "good" channel, early on in my practice I tried to immediately drop all of my boundaries and "aww shucks" my way into a connection with more "enlightened" beings from distant planes. All this got me was more firmly entrenched in my own intellect than I could imagine and as far away from connection with them as I could be. I gradually learned that in order to value others, especially others from different vibration levels, I had to value myself. It was very much like learning how to love on this plane. In order to love others, I had to first love and value myself. In fact, this was the very message Sanadaria had come to deliver through me to those who would listen. In order to love others you must first learn what it is to receive love. "You can't give what you don't have," she would tell people over and over again.

It was through Sanadaria that I first learned to consciously integrate new colors into my aura. I had previously been only vaguely aware of different aspects of the color spectrum and how they affected changes in my emotional body. I knew that colors could help people in the healing process, but I had yet to fully understand how the integration of colors can help raise vibration levels to experience more love. Sanadaria introduced my groups and me to the purple ray of unconditional love. "There are as many kinds of love in the universe as there are colors in the light spectrum—and more," she would say, "and yet the most beautiful hues are yet beyond your current capacity to view." Only when you fully learn to unselfconsciously open up your awareness to who you are will you begin to know this." I was reminded of all the different words the Eskimo tribes have for snow. It seemed I was to learn a new vocabulary—one not just of words, but of color and light.

Sanadaria often led groups in meditation, having us visualize an ultraviolet light, the purple ray, entering our bodies. "When you do this," she explained, you open yourselves up to the vibration of unconditional love that is the essence of my own being." In this way, she was sharing who she was with everyone in the room. Her presence was so touching to many in the group there were often tears in the eyes of those listening when they realized the truth of her words.

"This love," she continued," is not like the love of the third dimension, whose hand is taken away when you do not receive. Rather, it is like the hand of a lover gently caressing your face when it is your turn to receive and you are yet too tired to even turn away. Receive now, this love I have to give you, and allow all your fears to be placed into my hands, my hands that will gently melt away your fear to reveal the love that remains, the love that is yours. Trust and it will be so, trust and you will receive." We often joined hands and received this love together as a group. It did not diminish the individual uniqueness of the experience but served to better open up each of us to the love that was offered. We each received it in our own unique way, but how better to validate the experience than to feel it together.

Chapter 5

In Transition with Rocando

There were many days in the early part of my career when I felt weighed down by my own issues and challenges. It was during those days I began forming a deep and loving bond with the community of beings on the other side who are my guides. I would often talk with them as if they were sitting right beside me, and I have no doubt that many times they were. Sometimes while driving I would visualize a guide, Sananda perhaps, or Michael sitting in the passenger seat. It was, and still is, a vivid way for me to connect. They always give me the support in spirit never had in my physical life, especially in my childhood. It was because of this, I think, that I bonded so deeply with them.

As my work with the ascended masters grew, I began holding meetings in Missoula on a regular basis as well as in other towns where I had friends. It was common for my friends to invite people to their home to receive wisdom and guidance from the masters, my friends on the other side. I began calling the masters, "My group." As my ability to channel increased, the number of beings who showed up on the other side to be channeled increased, too. It was almost as if they were waiting for me to get up to speed with my spiritual gifts so I could be used by them. Still they would always tell me that my health and wellbeing were of paramount importance to them. They always cautioned me never to channel from a place of low energy or tiredness, ever admonishing me to use the cup-runneth-over theory. It still holds true today. It is also how I advise aspiring new channels.

In 1996, I sent in my first channeled article for publication to the *Sedona Journal of Emergence*. It was accepted, and my life has never been the same since. My writing/channeling for publication has led me to connections around the world, doing readings for people in most English speaking countries and in other countries for people who are bilingual. It has been the most rewarding experience of my life. It is beyond my ability to put into words how honored I feel to be of assistance to people on their spiritual path. It is at once fulfilling and humbling—ultimately my greatest joy. It gives me a sense of community not limited to things like political boundaries or religion. If only other people could see how we are all engaged in a search for what is true, pure, and innocent about ourselves there would be far less arguments and wars.

It was in 1996, 1997 and 1998, while bringing information to people throughout the U.S and beyond that I began putting a name to the group of beings I channeled. I called them Rocando, a name that was given to me during a particularly powerful channeling session. This group was comprised of all the individuals I had previously known by name and many more I had not yet met. I was told I could now channel the combined energies of about seventy-five beings from the other side. I could not identify them all, but could feel a growing awareness that I definitely was not alone.

I am frequently asked if working with the other side drains me. It is just the opposite. After working a full day or channeling for several hours, I might feel tired from holding a focus. I also feel energized and vibrant. If I work in the evening, it always takes me time to "come down" before I can fall asleep. It is an astounding sensation, almost as if I am still connected with a place in the universe that excels in love, peace, and contentment. Many times, I find myself feeling more drawn to that world than to this one.

Even though I didn't tire from the work, holding a concentrated focus for hours at a time was challenging for my body, especially in the beginning. I am a very physical person, one who thrives on exercise, and I found my body needing the balance of diet, exercise and sleep even more than ever. I also discovered to my delight that I was growing physically taller! It was as if my body was making changes to adapt to the new energy required for my work. The year I started channeling in earnest I grew almost an inch, and this was when I was in my forties! I went from a little under 5'8 to almost 5'9. I was delighted with the additional height. When I asked my guides about it they simply said, with their usual aplomb, "we needed you to be longer." I've always enjoyed being tall and have since asked for even more inches to be added to my "length," but apparently they are content with my 5'9 height.

I have read books by other channels and have often heard them speak of gaining weight after they agreed to be a channel, usually saying that their guides needed more weight to hold the energy in the physical dimension. After the fact, I found myself much relieved my guides added more to my body in height rather than in girth!

As I continued to channel and write, I began advertising in national magazines and was rewarded with many new clients. This was when I started to work internationally as well as nationally. I found people around the world, all working on the same personal issues. It filled me with a sense of awe to think that we are all here doing the same things: growing, learning, and healing. We are all in this together—another confirmation of the growing sense I had that we were all one. I knew this to be true.

The group Rocando was often a mischievous lot. They had a certain banter that was effective in rousing even the most stoic of listeners. They delighted in making puns and in making jokes about linear time. From their perspective, we must look very silly. They don't spare their hilarity on this and other aspects of humanity.

Once when an audience member asked a question about being on vacation; Rocando answered by saying, "Vacation, what is the purpose of this?" The audience member responded by saying it was for the purpose of relaxing and letting go of stress, getting out of old routines and habit patterns that no longer served him. The group then said, "Why is it you don't do this year-round and save worrying and stress for your two weeks a year?" Their response brought much laughter. It was always their way to joke people out of their entrenched ideas about what life is or should be.

The following text is a channeling from Rocando, as published in the *Sedona Journal of Emergence.* Notice how they refer to the people in the audience as "Masters." In their work with me, they unfailingly treat everyone with stature equal to their own. "How else could it be if we are indeed one?" they would always say. I could do nothing but concur.

You might also notice a certain sense of irreverence. It is something I have come to love about my group, their continued sense of humor. No matter how serious the questions are, they always respond with love and humor and at times, with downright silliness. It always bring us back into balance with what is really important and teaches us the age-old lesson that worry and fear are dissolved by laughter.

Many of the beings in the group are the masters described in Chapter One.

*　　　　　*　　　　　*

The Divine Body

January 14, 1998

Greetings, Masters. Tonight we will speak to you about the workings of the divine body. You might ask, "What is the divine body?" Why, it is your own physical being! It is the physical form you chose to inhabit in this lifetime. We call it the divine body simply because it is the instrument through which you hear the divine voice, feel the divine messages. It is how you connect with the divine in this third dimension. Ultimately, it is your instrument of peace.

Many of you have made the mistake of believing the body is sinful or corrupt, something to renounce or give up in the transition to wholeness, which is to say, the ascension process. This is not so. The body is just as divine as the soul that inhabits it. When you reject the body and all it has to offer you, you are rejecting a part of yourself the Divine One loves. Who are you to do this in your egos? You are loved for who you are, and your body is a part of that.

Though the physical body is not eternal—since it is a part of third dimension—it is nonetheless your vehicle through which you will manifest Divine Will and Divine Love in this domain. Because of this, the physical body needs to be honored equally as high as the spiritual part of you. There is consciousness in all parts of your physical body, whether you know it or not. In order to begin honoring your body, you must learn to communicate with it.

Communicating with your body is just as simple as talking to another person in your world. You must learn to open up a dialogue with your organs, your muscles, your cells, even with your brain itself. Did you know that you can even make contact with and talk to the enzymes in your body? Yes, most certainly you can. But the question is *will you*?

To begin discourse with your body, you must first find a level of acceptance for it. Many of you have bodies you do not like because of their shape or size. So instead of loving it, you reject it out of hand—We too are capable of puns, you know! Those of you who are what you would call "overweight" feel embarrassed about your bodies; you hide in clothes that do not show your physical form simply because of some ridiculous standard created back in your linear time called "Barbie." This is difficult for many of us to understand.

Is it that your species so lacks desire for diversity that you all try to conform to a rigid standard of what "should" be? Or is it that you so love the desire to create for yourselves the notion of love into a fixed form that you abandon your own being and its creativity when it does not fit the standard? Which is it? Why do you desire to be alike and talk of your need for individuality? You cannot do both. When you learn to love yourself *exactly as you are now,* you will see that your body has much love to give you in return. It is an honorable and loyal instrument for you to use, it has awareness of itself as a vehicle for the divine just as you do. Do not forsake your physical bodies; they have been bearing your consciousness for years, in ways far surpassing your understanding.

Consider allowing your notion of independence to include freedom from rigid thought. Why not try on the idea of embracing your uniqueness to the point that you revel in the joy of knowing that there is only one you? Soul, mind, and body—one you. One you, just as you are now, not as you might become in the future. There is only one *now,* you know.

So, you have embraced who you are and have found acceptance of yourself *as you are.* How do you now converse with your body and all its parts? Imagine your body to be a community of souls, or if you would rather, a community of beings. An organ such as your heart is actually made up of a diverse number of energies and beings, holding time within itself so that you may exist within linear time as an eternal being. It is an amazing feat, is it not? Imagine the balance it takes to beat sixty or seventy times *every minute* in exactly the same way. Now imagine doing that every minute, every hour, every day, for a hundred years or more! Is that not something worthy of your love? Your attention? Certainly you already give this group of energies your trust.

Who are the beings who make up the energies of your heart, who are doing this magnificent job for you? We will not answer that question for you. This is your job. It is your assignment, then, to find out for yourself who they are and why they so lovingly perform this service for you. You are in this together; isn't it high time you talked to your heart?

There are other services, of course, that your heart performs for you. We are not ignorant of the human heart being attributed with being the source of much emotion. This, too, is a role it plays. It allows you to love and be loved. What if your heart needed more love? Would you know it? If you open up a line of communication, you *will* know, because then your heart could speak to you.

Some of you hold back because you think it is foolish to talk to your body parts. Those of you holding this rigid thought pattern—and it is indeed rigid! —are the very ones who talk to your cars and your computers! If you spent only a fraction of the time talking to your body that you spend talking to machines, you would find your health and vitality improving along a scale that would soon go through the roof. Have you ever thought to consult your stomach about what it wants you to put into it? The stomach is not selfish as you might suppose; it takes a consensus about what is good for the whole organism and then communicates it to you. *It is there for your well being.* It even takes into account the emotions and what foods bring pleasure to you.

Some of you are afraid that if you begin talking to your stomachs you will never again be allowed to eat another chocolate doughnut! Come now. Is not a divergence from pure health, what you might call a splurge or an occasional midnight snack, in order now and then? If it is good for the soul, it is often good for the whole body. Sometimes you *must* eat simply for the pure pleasure of it. You are a sensual being are you not? The senses must be pleased as well as the other parts of you. You must *all* learn to work together for the good of the whole: body, mind, and spirit.

Many of you and your publications often teach about the balance between body, mind, and spirit. But why is it you elevate the last two and leave the body to take care of itself? Your organs have emotional needs too, you know. Your kidneys need love; your pineal needs light; your mind needs stimulation. So much of this you take for granted. What if your heart decided to take a break for the day? Where would that leave your spirit? That's right, you'd have an immediate out of body experience—a rather permanent one!

We jest with you but only to illustrate a point. Many of the processes that occur within your body—things that honor and support your need for third-dimensional experience—are the result of a complex series of connections between energies and beings that you can't even begin to understand with your intellect. The body is made up of millions, rather billions, of connections, cooperative projects, creative processes and energies all coming together in a unified field of energy that is "you." A divine idea, divine cooperation, a divine Oneness, right there in third dimension!

Yes, a divine Oneness. You all desire Oneness with the divine. So we tell you, why not begin being a part of the divine Oneness that is your *body*, mind, and spirit? We know you will eventually do this, for ascension is impossible without it. It is just a matter of time. Why not let that time be now?

Many of you have learned to speak to your "inner child." This is an admirable thing. It is a true affirmation of the creativity, imagination, and emotions working together. You have, many of you, formed a bond with this child, have you not? Why not with the other parts of yourself then? Why not with your liver, your pancreas, your skin? They also desire acceptance, nurturing. They are not different from you; all of it is you.

Once you begin opening up the lines of communication with all parts of yourself, you will find a beauty of diversity within that is equaled only by the diversity without—in races, species, sexes, and so on. In this diversity is the divine plan made manifest. Beauty through diversity creates strength. Beauty through acceptance of diversity creates Oneness, Oneness of what is.

Honoring your body's needs is a way of loving yourself, you the *whole* being, in a way you can only understand and feel when it happens. It is a giving thing. It is also a freeing thing. The freedom you will find in these interchanges will inspire your spirit to soar to new heights with love you only dared imagine. It will be self-love, formed in the essence of who you are in your divine self. It will be the experience of divine self-love on many levels.

There is also much wisdom to be gleaned from the body and the records it keeps of your past lifetimes. Yes, your cells and their DNA have records, images, and memories of many things from your past. This can benefit you. Your body is a rich source of knowledge.

Your body as a whole is a fine instrument of discernment. How often have you been in a situation where your stomach, your "gut feeling," tells you the truth when no one else will? Your body will not lie to you like other humans do. It has no interest in doing so. The whole would not benefit from such action. Think about this the next time you want to put "garbage" into your stomach without asking it.

In the discernment your body offers you, is the exacting information about your life that you have always wanted to perceive. This is why it is so beneficial for you to learn to understand all of the sweet nuances, the subtle prompting your body offers you. Think of the world's great psychics and healers. They do their work with all of who they are. They note delicate differences in people's energies not just with their eyes and ears, but with their hands, feet, spine, and heart. Their bodies are like finely tuned instruments, speaking to them in rhapsodies of information flowing through their hearts and minds—a Oneness of communication.

To hear the body and all its parts, you must *feel* what it says to you; you must intuit its input on a feeling level. You all know what it is like to get a gut feeling. It is like this with all things of the body. Feel them the way you do that. Practice doing this, and you will become proficient at it long before you would expect to. We—and your own guides—are there to encourage and teach you how. It will take practice, and it will take discipline, but if you simply remind yourself to talk to some part of your body as if it were a person, your body will respond to you in its own language—the language of feelings.

Becoming aware of feelings for many of you is still a difficult thing. Your overactive intellects often take control and run roughshod over your emotions. Be gentle in the transition to feeling your emotions; allow yourself time to come to a place where it is safe for you to do this. For many of you, this will involve finding a confidant, a close friend who does not judge you when you share how you feel. It is important you do this now. There are many new abilities humankind is opening up to, and all of these abilities have at their foundation an ability to feel emotion through all parts of the body, not just through the heart.

This is why it is so important you learn to talk to your body. But in order to do so, you must first learn its language. There is information encoded in your cells. When the time is right, your cells from every place within you will open up and give you the keys to the kingdom of heaven. You have already been told, "The kingdom is heaven is within." What did you suppose this meant? It was not just a platitude. You hold the keys to the kingdom, and you hold them in a place they cannot be taken away from you. You hold them in your cells.

Your cells have all knowledge. Your DNA *is* the divine blueprint; it is the divine plan for the planet. It is the divine you, the divine body! Do you see? Do you *now* want to talk to you body? Then learn its language. Learn how to quiet the mind long enough to listen to what your body has to say. Each cell has a piece of the puzzle. They are all working together for the greater good. Even the mind itself will speak to you; though the mind is a chatterbox that loves itself in such a narcissistic way that it will never cease its babbling unless you ask it to. But do so lovingly, as you would with your heart.

What else do you need to know? Talking to the body is like talking to God, but then the body *is* God, is it not? Do you see this now? The body is not God to the exclusion of the rest of you because all of you *is* God. So then, talking to body is like talking to God: It is good to speak, it is even better to listen. That is where the wisdom is gained. It takes patience, persistence, and loving attention to listen

Listen to the body as if it were a young child who has been told to be quiet over and over again. This child has grown hesitant, and its speech is faltering at times, so you must be patient. But, much like the inner child, once the child feels your loving acceptance and approval, once it comes to know that its voice is honored and valued, it learns to trust, to feel and share those feelings. In the coming times, these feelings will be the lifeblood of unity and of Oneness. Embrace yourself, all of yourself. You hold the keys; use them wisely.

Chapter 6

Sananda

I think I have always preferred the name Sananda to Jesus, though this wise master still goes by both. I think it's because it allows me to see so much more of him as a master than just who he was in that one lifetime. Since organized religion has always felt limiting to me, it is helpful too for me to see that Sananda exists beyond this dogma. Many of my clients still refer to him as Jesus though, and that is just fine with me. My personal preferences are just that, my own.

Sananda became a close ally in my search for more wisdom from the other side. He was sometimes a companion, sometimes a friend, and always a master. I often had the feeling he was with me, patiently watching me grow into the teacher I was to become. He never judged me or even criticized me in those early days; none of them ever did. I was so hyper-sensitive and self-doubting, I don't think I could have stood it.

His close attention to my needs grew into a loving bond between us. Though I know we are all loved, I'm never completely sure what they think about us from the other side. I knew Sananda cared mostly by the way he just sat and listened. It was what I needed most, a friend. He was all that and much more. Even though I was not lacking for companionship on this side of the veil there was a part of me reaching out so fervently for the intimacy of spirit that there was little anyone physical could offer me in this quest.

Sananda gave me that intimacy. It was as if he was there for me in a way I couldn't have asked him to be because many times, I didn't even know what I needed. Still he was there. I channeled Sananda often in those early days, and doing so always filled me with love. Whenever I channeled him, I felt so much more than the words we spoke together, and this still holds true. It was like being filled up with love, and the words spoken to the groups was the love spilling over onto others. I began to experience the meaning of "My cup runneth over."

With my channeling abilities strengthening, I lost much of my self-doubt. I relaxed and the result was the ability to bring through humor. The masters are not just wise, but funny as all get out when they want to be. In fact, I still find humor to be one of the greatest tools for teaching. It is also when I feel the most profound love from my friends in the ethers. To describe it, I would have to say it's like when you are with a close friend and they give you a hard time, knowing you will laugh and not take it personally. The best way I can illustrate this is to tell a story from my own relationship with them.

Often, even when I was busy with groups or clients, I was immersed in my own personal growth issues. I, too, struggle with many of the things my clients come to me for: fear of the future, insecurity, even past issues from my own childhood. It was just after I had come to a realization of great import, feeling even a little smug that I had identified an old pattern that no longer served me. I was ready to give it up and move on. It was with this arrogance I went to my guides and asked them, "Hey, I found an old pattern, I can now let go of, isn't that right?"

Their immediate response was not in words. They simply showed me the picture of a dinosaur! Instead of being offended, I roared with laughter. It was indeed an obvious thing, and one that had taken me quite some time to identify. At times like these, when I grew through my own tough issues, I learned to laugh at myself.

It is often difficult to describe what my communication with the ascended masters is like. It isn't like what you would call an everyday experience. When I am with them connecting for a client or meditating on something myself, it's often like I live between worlds. Not completely immersed in theirs and certainly not limited to mine. It's like having a telephone line to God in a way. I never doubt that I am loved and though I go through periods of difficulty, I always know there is really nothing to fear.

When I "tune-in" for someone else, it's almost as if I shed the barriers between myself and the other side. I can feel them with me and in doing so feel complete. It doesn't solve my challenges of this life, but it does let me know I am not alone. It is this feeling of not being alone that I think helps others to heal. Most people can handle many challenges if they are not alone when they do so. Fears are so much easier to face in the company of a friend or guide.

When I'm channeling a guide or master there is a blending of our two beings, our consciousness. It's a warm feeling of being loved beyond all doubt, beyond all reason to doubt. It's what I call "knowing that I know." Along with this knowing comes a sense of being outside of linear time. At times I feel as if the clock doesn't move one second, like I am suspended beyond what we call time. Still in other times with the guides, I could swear that a single moment lasted an hour. Maybe this is due to the intensity of the connection.

The most intriguing facet of my connection with the guides is their ability to "download" me with information in a split second that takes me several minutes to communicate or explain to another. At times it's as if I gain the complete understanding of chapter of a book in an instant. And that's not all. While I am given this download of information, in an instant I sense and feel what my client is feeling and also "feel" an understanding of the situation from the guides, often impossible to communicate in words. It's a feeling like being able to *be* my guide and feel what they feel. It is this aspect of the connection I enjoy the most in my work.

In the early days of my work, Sananda was my favorite guide to channel. My trust for him was absolute. I knew he would never harm me or take me some place where I would be overwhelmed either with my own issues and feelings or a client's. I'd had some religious training in church and knew Sananda as "Jesus," but back then I often felt I was trying to worship God in a box. The dogma of the church seemed so limiting it left me cold.

I had a much more intimate connection with Sananda that didn't include worrying about going to hell or being judged for what I was doing. I know churches do stress that we are loved, especially by Jesus, but I never felt that love so strong as when I knew I was not limited to worshipping him as Jesus, the man or Jesus, the son of God. To me he was simply my friend who sat with me and listened to me in all my states, in all places, and in all beliefs. He could talk to people through me regardless of their beliefs or religion and give them peace. Theirs was not a religious connection and neither was mine.

One of the things I enjoy most about my friends in the spirit realm is their ability to cut right to the heart of the matter without beating around the bush. It was like when they showed me the picture of the dinosaur; they usually used the same directness with my clients. I once channeled Sananda for a woman in a telephone session and after she received the tape recording of our session, she wrote down some of the one sentence words of wisdom Sananda spoke to her. If brevity is the essence of wit then certainly it is also the soul of wisdom. Here is the list she sent me. It is Jesus who speaks:

"How effortless everything in life can be. Like it is Christmas every day. If you do not open all your gifts each day, they will pile up.

It is a certainty that life is a never-ending gift.

Accept all emotions. Fear of not being in control of one's life is what aging is about.

Take time to experience joy in all things.

Abandon the idea that anything will be difficult.

Everything you embody is being taught to others by virtue of your actions: being who you are.

We fear because of self-doubt.

We are loved unconditionally. When we presuppose that we are not loved, every thing changes. We go about trying to prove we are loveable when we already are.

Meditation as a discipline is overrated.

Life is a meditation on love.

Love transcends fear and permeates it. It draws everything in linear time away from itself and into bliss.

Simply trust yourself.

Self-acceptance is the gateway to the watershed of love.

Trust that what you cannot see nor affect will come to you.

There is no death; it is a joke.

You must become like a child to enter heaven. Children are not concerned about acceptance or judgment

It is okay to love everybody.

It is true that we are all one.

My love is with you always."

My personal favorites are the last three. They seem to sum up all we ever need to know about life.

When spiritual connection is made across the dimensions, small differences in our humanity or choices of expression become so small as to be meaningless. It is only when we fear who we are that we find ourselves mistrusting others or rejecting parts of ourselves. That is how we often block the unconditional love of our guides, angels and the ascended masters.

Some of the most sensitive and touching messages Sananda ever gave others through me were messages of love and acceptance so complete that he went to the greatest lengths of his being to align himself with them right where they lived. I once asked him about this, this business of how he almost slips out of his own identity as an individual to reach out to others—certainly going beyond how many of them knew him as Jesus.

In his response to me about this, he compared himself to a chameleon. "I like to disappear into the act of helping someone, so they don't see me but see only what they need to receive. This makes it easier for them to receive the help they need."

Always the invisible guest, Sananda's presence is often with me when I am not aware of him, though I have been told by my friends this is so. This does not bother me, in fact quite the contrary, it makes me able to focus on what I am thinking and feeling so I can get past whatever obstacles are in front of me.

Ever-humble, Sananda is always ready to reach out a helping hand. I have even watched him smile at how people don't see him but see only the action of love entering a situation. How often have you prayed for a solution only to find one entering your mind without knowing how it got there? Perhaps you have met this master of humility smiling his way past you unseen.

Sananda makes himself available to the common person in every situation. I have seen him align himself with people from many varied religions, not always Christian. He seems not to care if you receive him or believe in him, much to the contrary of what Christian religions would have us believe. Concerning this mandate from the religious world, he says, "I hold no hope of being God to everyone. This is impossible, everyone is different in personality, culture, beliefs. It is enough for me to simply love everyone. Believe what you will, and I will always love you."

Patience is also a strong trait of Sananda's. He will wait an eternity for you to understand a simple concept. Unlike Kuthumi or St. Germain, whose role it seems is to hammer away at the intellect until it yields to your open heart and you understand something with your feelings that your head cannot grasp. Sananda is always lovingly companionable, ever ready to just hang out with you. I think he liked life here and wants to interact with those of us who invite him to do so once again.

I have seen Sananda touch clients of mine from almost every walk of life. His love knows no judgment. Whatever your gender, religion, race, sexual orientation, occupation, or belief system, Sananda is ready to see your life from your perspective, not his. He will show you how he could be all of these things with you and love sharing them with you. His love knows no bounds such as these. It often amazes me to see how much joy it gives him in aligning with you right where you live. This is how he shows us his love for us the most, by being like us and showing us how perfect we are just as we are. He would not change a hair on our heads.

It is the fabric of who Sananda is to give of himself in this way, so I would like to illustrate just how he does this. I once channeled Sananda for a young woman who had been abused by her mother. This woman, who I will call Melissa, was wrestling with hatred and anger towards her mother that was the result of child abuse and neglect. She also held resentment about the abuse and neglect of her younger brother.

Melissa's mother was no longer living, but she hated her all the same. Being religious and a Christian, Melissa had a tough time accepting her feelings of anger and rejection, which were natural reactions to an abusive parent. Her religion, of course, taught forgiveness, but without first healing the pain, the timing of forgiveness was inappropriate.

I'd worked with for Melissa for some time and found myself unable to assist her in finding self-acceptance. Since Melissa was religious, I hesitated to channel for her but had always remained in my own personality giving what counsel I could. It was not enough and I knew it. Struggling with how to give her more, I asked my guides for help. Immediately, I was told to simply relax and allow Sananda to speak.

The night we spoke, Melissa had been crying and feeling the pain of the past, especially about her brother for whom she could do nothing. I did as my guides requested, stepping aside to let the master come through. I held my breath, hoping I would not be pronounced a fraud, or worse. What transpired amazed me. When Sananda spoke to Melissa he was gentle but firm. I do not have a tape of this conversation, but I remember it went something like this:

Sananda said, "Be still my child, it is I, Jesus and I have come to comfort you."

With no hesitation, Melissa fell into step with Sananda saying, "Oh Jesus, I need you so much, I can't help hating my mother for what she did. I know I'm wrong, but it hurts so much that I just can't let go of it."

"I am with you, and I hurt with you," Sananda said.

Melissa began speaking in a child-like voice, and I was certain she was reliving some difficult memories, "I wanted so much to help him, she sobbed, "our mother locked him in a closet and he was only nine years old! I hate her I hate her!" As the childhood anger and pain poured out, I found my arms around her with Sananda's energy pouring through me. Sananda was giving her all the support she could receive, and I felt she knew he was there.

As she continued to cry, Sananda spoke the ultimate words of forgiveness and consolation, "I understand my child, I hate her too for what she did!"

"You do?" Melissa asked, sitting up with an astonished look on her face.

With a crooked little half-smile she said, "You do?" I saw a great wave of relief sweep through her body, and she relaxed into the chair beneath her.

"Yes, I do," Sananda said. "How could anyone not? The two of you did not deserve what you received."

Melissa accepted this truth automatically. I could sense the pieces falling into place for her. Her guilt about feeling hatred and anger was gone, as was her pain. "Yeah, I know," she said with new conviction. She nodded numbly, at peace with all that had just occurred.

I asked her later what she thought of the incident, the conversation with Sananda, or Jesus, as she knew him. She said she knew she had received a miracle. Though her church would have probably pronounced me a heretic, Melissa had no doubt. She had spoken with her Lord and had been healed. She was now at peace.

Many times, the guides, not just Sananda but all of them, have ways of assisting us that are so far beyond my understanding, I can only stand back in awe and watch the masters at work. I have often seen Sananda go to the very limit of someone's fear, anger or pain with them to demonstrate how they are not alone and how completely they are encompassed in loving arms. I have no doubt of this love. It is the ultimate compassion.

When Sananda spoke of how he too hated Melissa's mother, it was, of course, her mother's behavior he hated and not the person herself but in a strange way the words he spoke to Melissa were exactly what she needed to hear. They contained the validation, love, and forgiveness she could not give herself.

Whenever I think about Sananda, or Jesus, as many of my clients still call him, I *always* feel loved. His presence to me is like a clear mountain stream that never stops flowing, and I know it never will. Though Sananda was my first real support from the other side, he is by no means my greatest connection. That is reserved for two very special beings you will read about in later chapters. Still, he remains my friend, playmate and ever-present companion, always ready to help me—or anyone in need. I know my understanding of him is so very limited that I can only hope to someday, perhaps from the other side myself, come to know more of who he is.

Chapter 7

St. Germain

St. Germain has been an interesting and intriguing being for me to channel. Sometimes it pure delight and fun. He is as light and airy as any of the etheric beings I know, and yet his earthiness almost belies his existence in spirit. He is as down-to-earth, funny and sardonic as they come. He invites criticism, revels in disorder, and will laugh you right out of your foul mood and sour disposition. While being channeled, he often asks the audience if they have any good jokes to tell and will tell you a few of his own. Though in truth (St. Germain, forgive me for saying this), he doesn't quite have all the nuances of earthly humor down. And perhaps this is the point; he often leads us perilously close to our own foibles so we can laugh at ourselves. So watch out if you begin to take yourself too seriously; an afternoon with St. Germain will leave you uprooted and uncertain of your old footing.

I began to understand Germain's humor when I started teaching a regular Thursday night meditation class in Kalispell. Each evening, about a dozen of us would gather to meditate and receive whatever guidance came through. It was in one of these classes that I first saw St. Germain put someone through his paces. It was one of my meditation students, and he was all intellect. Sandy was an extremely loving and big hearted man but valued his intelligence above all else. This kept him from receiving much of the guidance through his heart. It wasn't that he was cold or uncaring, far from it. He was warm and encouraging to others, supportive and inquisitive. He had an exceptionally strong desire to learn meditation, but he couldn't get past his brain. I suspected underneath the sharp mind was soft spot but also a fear of being vulnerable enough to let anyone get too close.

Sandy also had a need to "prove" the existence of things instead of accepting them on faith. Though a man of great faith in God, Sandy would often ask that things be proven to him instead of relying on his own faith and discernment. Comments from Germain like "Trust that is so," would often send Sandy spiraling up into the world of thought instead of that of spirit. Asking for proof of things in the spirit world is like asking someone to describe why a sunset looks as it does. It can be done, but it takes all the poetry out of it. This was Germain's forte.

Germain would often lead Sandy down a path of supreme intellectual debate only to let Sandy get all tangled up in the depth of his own mind long enough to let go. As with others who have a hard time leaving the intellect, Sandy would eschew emotions and trust what he could think about instead of feel. With many of my clients, this is usually the result of difficult emotions they would rather not feel. Letting go of control is often a large part of this. Still I found Sandy and Germain's conversations to be great lessons in tolerance, perseverance, and love. Germain's acceptance of Sandy and his ability to work with him was by far the greatest measure of acceptance I was to find.

Sandy used his keen intellect to banter with St. Germain. Germain, not to be outdone, would take Sandy on a journey through intellect and right on into spirit with the greatest of ease. Though I do not have any of their conversations taped, I witnessed enough of their conversations to give you a good idea of what they were like. They often went something like this:

Sandy: So how do we really know you are who you say you are?

Germain: You don't.

Sandy: Then how can we trust what you tell us, how can we rely on you or even believe you exist?

Germain: *You* can't but others do my friend. They *feel* the truth of it.

Sandy: But isn't that subjective?

Germain: Indeed it is! What is your truth?

Sandy: What do you mean?

Germain: How do you arrive at what is true for you? How do you know what choices to make and so on?

Sandy: Hmm.

Germain: You see, my friend, it is always easier to test than to love.

Sandy: How else do you arrive at what is true?

Germain: You receive the truth, you don't prove what is true. You can not understand spirit in the intellect. When you are willing to receive truth, you will understand.

Sandy: Isn't that a catch-22?

Germain: Indeed it is, and it is your mind that is caught in the trap of third dimension. You see, the third dimension will always give you more and more opportunity to analyze, judge, criticize, and proclaim the almighty truth of the intellect. But spirit will boldly ask you to trust what you feel. It is in this that wisdom is found. Intellectual truth is not always wise. Which would you rather have, a chocolate bar (Sandy's favorite!) or the recipe for chocolate? One is right, the other is yummy.

Sandy: That's irrelevant. Why can't I have both? I can understand what chocolate is and eat it too, can't I?

Germain: Yes indeed, but which would you prefer? If you didn't understand what ingredients were in this delicious treat, would you enjoy it less? Would you still *trust* it was safe to eat?

Sandy: That's not a fair analogy I still think I can do both.

Germain: Yes, my friend, but which feels better? It is so with the world of feelings and of spirit. You can go about your whole life wondering why something is so, or you can partake of it. Your mind is like the proverbial steel trap, sharp and decisive. But still a trap in which *you* are caught. The mind is like the recipe for chocolate. It has power to understand but also the power to separate you from your feelings and senses of the world. There are many powerful things in the world, and I tell you the truth, the emotions are more powerful than the mind. You are not your mind. You are spirit, and your feelings can lead you to experience this.

When you want to stir someone into action, do you not touch their emotions? When you want to receive something from someone, do you not touch their heart? Where would you rather be touched, in your mind or in your heart? Let your heart lead you my friend, and it will take you to the taste of chocolate and to the taste of spirit.

It is at this point, Sandy would usually give in, either by feeling things within his heart and get teary, or tiring of it all, change the subject. I have seen St. Germain do this with many people, much to their dismay and mortification. You cannot talk Germain out of anything. You can only get confused and shift to your feelings, become willing to give up control, or stay stuck in the trap of the intellect. The guides have often told me that not all people will be able to be guided to their hearts in this lifetime.

It interesting to me that most of the people who have a hard time letting go of the mind usually request to speak to St. Germain themselves. I always chuckle to myself when this happens. They have no idea what they are getting themselves in to. As I channel, I sit back and watch with awe the master at work. I think the clients who request him must think they are getting away with something, but landing right in the lap of St. Germain is not what the expect.

St. Germain was one of the original masters I got to know early on in my channeling career, and I was often intimidated by the encounters. I realized, in retrospect, it was not Germain I feared but the people who showed up for the channeling sessions with wanting "proof" of what was happening. Proof of the existence of God, or of ascended beings and angels here to help us, falls easily under the old adage, "If you don't believe no proof is enough; if you do believe no proof is necessary."

The intellect will never be satisfied with answers that come from this world or the world of Spirit. It is simply a matter of being willing to believe and then being willing to be led to the intimate "proof" that touches your own heart in such a way as to bring you peace or love. In my years of working in the field of teaching psychic awareness and spirituality, I have never known it to be otherwise. I have come to understand though that willingness often holds the key.

The willingness to believe is often the only place one can start. If you are willing to believe what is true in your heart, your heart can receive. It is open. If you are unwilling to let go and receive a truth about Spirit or about yourself then you will, with the help of God, let go. Often it is not our own ability that allows us to receive but the openness and willingness to do so. I have found so often with myself or with countless others that it is the willingness to let go that allows us to receive the help we need in order to do so.

Letting go of fear, doubt, or hurt is like holding onto a live wire with electricity running through it. It is an old pattern that has become so reinforced through too many years of our use, we have become entrenched in it. When we ask for help in letting go, a power beyond us can come to our aid.

Often when working with clients, they express sadness when they finally realize they want to let go but cannot. In many ways, this is the beginning of wisdom and the start of the spiritual path. It is where the client finally sees the need to ask for help and also sees the need to surrender in order to receive that help. The willingness to begin this process is is the action that is needed to begin. This is when all aid rushes to your side.

St. Germain often brings many people to this very point. To the place where they admit their minds cannot take them to the peace they desire. That peace can only be found in the heart. Germain has said it like this:

"When desire is felt for peace, allow it some latitude and do not force it. Do not say to it, "Go that way, come to me this way." No, peace is as illusive as a fragrance in the wind. First you sense it near and then it is gone. When you chase it, you create such a wind yourself, it rushes away from you. But if you sit quietly and breathe in the life around you, all beauty comes to you. All of your senses are attuned to this, not merely your mind. Your mind is just what allows you to get by in the world. Things like doing math, driving your car and reading books, this is what the intellect is for. Peace is the small voice in your spirit, in your heart, that cries out for rest. It is the part of you that wants to come home to God. Let it be so. Let yourself come home to rest. It is in this quest we offer you assistance.

"This is the quest for the Holy Grail, the quest for peace within. It is not found in a chapter of a book nor in a journey to a distant place. It is found only near the still small voice within you. The voice that says, 'I give up, I can walk no farther without grace. I must learn to receive. I *must* receive. I am willing to receive! Help me now.'

"We stand ready to assist you, great beings of light. Join us in the quest. In this we are one! It is not a quest that allows you to arrive at a destination. It is a journey of ever-increasing joy and fulfillment. One that honors you as you honor it. In the quest for peace there is only love and soon you will all partake of it. Those of you who are willing to let down your guard and receive will indeed receive. You will receive the gifts of joy and love and of honoring who you are.

Open your hearts to love. Many of you have lived so long in your intellects that you do not truly know what love is. Let love draw you to itself. Let love guide you to your own heart. Let love be the only motivation for you to follow. Let it lead you to your heart so you may receive from us and from what you call God. God is the unity of all souls in eternal love and bliss. Come home to this love. It is your birthright and your heritage. It is the dance of life that will lead you here. Let your own desire lead you to the peace your heart yearns for. Come home to love. Indeed, let us go home together."

Chapter 8

Archangel Michael

It was October of 1997, and I was in a booth at a New Age fair. A woman in her late thirties, whom I will call Celeste, walked in and sat down to have a reading. She seemed a bit nervous, which I had come to know is quite common. Most people before a reading exhibit some degree of nervousness. Never quite sure what they will be told, they almost hold their breath waiting to find out what the guides have to say.

As I relaxed into my chair, I was filled with a sense of "this is going to be a powerful reading." I closed my eyes and Archangel Michael appeared to me in my mind, letting me know he was ready to begin. This in itself is not unusual, Michael always announces himself to me in this fashion, asking my permission before he comes in to be channeled. Usually, he "stands" behind or next to me, sometimes tapping me on the shoulder with his energy in his respectful and gentle way, saying, "I am ready whenever you are." The image I describe belies the strength of his energy and though he could in all probability force me to channel him, he never has. This time, though, his words were direct and precise. (I have heard him announce himself in this manner many times since.) He said, "Move over! I have something I have to say to this woman!"

Michael's demanding tone did not ruffle me. After intimately knowing him for some time now, I had complete faith and trust in him. Though he was forceful, I still felt an abiding sense of peace. So, I "stepped aside" to allow Michael to come in, and he began one of the most loving exchanges I have ever heard him engage in. His presence was like a warm river that flowed smoothly together with my own life force. He brought comfort, love and reassurance. I could feel all of it. Michael began to speak.

"My dearest being of light. Time has come for you to allow all the blessings we have for you to flow into your life. You have labored long and hard to please others, now it is time to receive for yourself. We have a plan for you that will make you very happy. There are changes you must make to allow all to come into alignment with your great purpose. That purpose is love. Let me explain."

Michael then began telling her of a great love that awaited her, a great and eager soul mate. He told her that this man already loved her so much he would swim across the oceans to get to her if need be. As Michael continued, I found myself welling up with emotion and Celeste was already wiping tears off her cheeks. The beauty of the love he described to her was beyond anything I had heard described or seen on Earth in any relationship. It was divine love in human form, and Michael did not want her to miss out on it.

They continued to speak. Michael insisted that the time had come for Celeste to receive love. He began speaking to her of her faith. She had faith that would move mountains. She believed with all her heart that if she stood in her faith and gave lovingly to those who were most important in her life, she would be provided for as well. In this belief system, however, there was no room for her to receive.

As they interacted, I found myself feeling the love Michael was describing. It was a deep and constant devotion that would not only serve each partner but would ultimately serve love itself. Since then, I have come to know this love is the destiny for us all. As we serve each other in love, we become closer to God, serving God as well. As we serve God, we serve the Earth and ourselves. This is the approaching oneness of love we all hear about. I am certain the more we love each other, the more love excels in the Earth and abounds for us all.

As Michael was speaking to Celeste, I began to become aware of an unusual sensation, something I had not experienced in my channeling. For some reason, Michael seemed to be drawing me closer to the conversation almost as if he wanted me to listen in and receive something for myself. I edged my way into a deeper awareness of what was being said and saw how profound the message was. How few people are given this message of waiting love? I was sure Celeste was happy. As I continued to listen more closely, I found Michael shifting his "gaze" to me. He began telling me that I was to expect to receive the same love from a waiting partner!

I was shocked. Being single for many years, I had often thought of meeting a man for whom I could feel an unconditional and have that love returned as well. It seemed Michael was giving me confirmation of this desire! I was stunned and could not hold back a few tears of my own—tears of joy. Profoundly touched, I finished the session with Celeste and shared with her what Michael had told me. We both sat in silence for some time. Then after a few moments, Celeste began to explain just how extraordinary Michael's message to her was.

Regaining her composure, Celeste told me she was married with two children. I immediately thought to question the information she was given and doubt myself. This woman was a complete stranger to me; perhaps I had allowed the wrong information to be given out. No, I thought again, the connection was too strong, too powerful, there could be no mistake. I listened to Celeste continue to talk. She told me she had already been informed by another psychic that she would be getting divorced. She wasn't unhappy, but certainly not fulfilled, and it was only her selfless heart of faith that kept her serving her family in the purest of devotion.

She adored her children and cared for her husband but the relationship had lost its joy, its life.

Michael knew Celeste was not happy. He was simply letting her know her time of hardship was coming to an end. As Celeste continued to speak with me, what came was out how she had selflessly given herself to her children and husband of some twenty years. She was spent, exhausted and in need of change. This she knew. Now she also knew what awaited her. She felt Michael's words to be true, for her there was no doubt. What she still wondered was how it all would come about. At that moment, I felt Michael come to me once again, "Trust," he said to her. Celeste left me with a feeling of serenity on her face. I sensed her interaction with Michael was too big to be put aside or forgotten.

I doubted not a word of what Michael said to her, or to me, when he included me in the message that I feel was always intended for both of us. As I write this, I have not yet met the man who would swim an ocean to be with me, but I don't doubt I will.

I usually never hear what transpires for a client, especially when meeting in a fair. People go on with their lives not knowing that I sometimes wonder what happens to them. With Celeste it was different. About a year and a half later, perhaps two, I had a call from her. Many things had changed in her life. She and her husband had separated amicably, and her children were in the process of adjusting. She was calling because she had met someone new, her soul mate and wanted confirmation. I was happily able to tell her, "Yes, this is the man Michael had spoken of that day." It was one of the best callbacks I ever received.

I've channeled Archangel Michael many times, though the first time I met him was unlike any encounter I had up to that point. It was in my office during my regular Thursday night group that he made his first appearance to me. I was seated in my wooden rocking chair, the chair I always used for readings and groups. The audience that night was small, seated in a circle. It was quiet in the room as I waited to receive guidance for the evening.

I felt a presence enter the room and someone came and stood behind my chair. I felt a weight pressing on me, almost leaning into me. It wasn't a physical pressure but an energy of enormous proportion. I sensed that a very tall and powerful being was leaning all of his five hundred pounds of energy against my back and asking to come in to be channeled! I asked the audience if anyone knew who was here. I often gave my students a chance to identify beings who made an appearance in spirit to help them learn to identify different energies. In the beginning of my channeling career, I used this as confirmation for myself, too. Two women both immediately knew it was Michael.

Michael is often identified by other channels as strong, mighty, and even stern. This is undoubtedly a side of Michael that exists, but it is never how he has come to me. That night, it was as though a warm and flowing river of unconditional love flowed into me. Michael was able to meld his energy with my own and give me his strength. It was a new and exciting way of feeling loved: gentle and affirming, strong, and absolutely unwavering. This sense of unwavering dedication is how I know Michael best. "My sweet protector" I call him.

Not yet familiar with Michael, I found myself asking for clarity and for confirmation that only the highest good of all present be honored. I felt a sense of tranquillity flood into me as a response and I marveled at how effortless the connection with this power being was. It was simple, as Michael told me, "you just open up your arms and embrace me with your whole heart." It was like receiving a tender yet powerful hug from someone I had known long before. I felt like I was reconnecting with an old friend, one I trusted absolutely. I knew all this in the instant Michael made contact with me. There was no struggle with this, no doubt; the love Michael gave me that night left no room for uncertainty.

I've had many experiences with Michael in times when I felt unsafe in the world. Once while visiting a friend in a city in the east, I took a walk into town and, misjudging the time, found myself walking back in the dark. A small-town person at heart, I do not feel completely comfortable on dark city streets. As I quickened my pace, I felt a growing feeling of anxiety at my vulnerability. I quickly checked in with Michael, and whoosh, he was at my side. In subsequent experiences, I have come to understand that he is usually with me before I realize it, protecting me while I worry needlessly. In this case, I felt immeasurably better when Michael made his presence known to me in such a vivid way and got home without incident. His comfort and protection always puts me at my ease.

On another occasion, I was working with a client who was facing some difficult childhood issues of neglect and abandonment. She was feeling alone and vulnerable, too. As I tuned-in to see how to help her, Michael came through to tell her he would assist. She expressed her fear of being vulnerable and open. He said to her, "I will stand with my back to your back and make sure no one comes to harm you. My client suddenly broke down into tears. Unknown to me, she had often been betrayed as a child by those she loved. Michael saw this clearly and showed her how he would not allow this to happen again. My client later told me she could physically feel Michael's back against her own.

It is Michael's strength I see most often in my work with him, his loving protection for myself, and others. After the incident in the city at night, I have never again felt alone and vulnerable, knowing Michael is always with me.

I am often asked how Michael and others can be with so many people around the world at once. I am at a loss to explain how this can be. There are so many things in this world that defy description and even understanding. As St. Germain says, it is not the intellect that holds these and other answers for us. The heart has its own way with things of the spirit, things we cannot understand with all the brainpower at our command. When I think of Michael's power, I often think of the Grand Canyon. We can see it, but cannot take it all in. Those who can feel the power of the Canyon are silenced by it and sit quietly gazing into its depth.

They enter a secret world that is not of the mind nor of the third dimension. This dimension is only a gateway to love and to the myriad of other realities that exist alongside the world we live in. What we see in nature is often what we see in ourselves.

When we are willing to admit that we contain love, we contain the universe, and we contain creation in our hearts, we can then begin to glimpse the power of beings like Michael. It is only then we can imagine that we too are worthy of receiving love from him and others like him. He, too, is just a gateway to other ways of understanding God and understanding that God is within us. I know of no way to justify or explain this to the questioning mind.

Chapter 9

Djwal Khul

There is another being whose energy is akin to Kuthumi, and that is Djwal Khul, or affectionately, DK. I was channeling Djwal Khul for a young man in California when I noticed the similarity. I used my technique of having an aside conversation with the master while DK was answering questions for my client over the phone.

As I was sensing the similarity between he and Kuthumi, I asked him why he seemed so much the same as the Kuthumi, the one they call, world teacher. He told me that although they resonate with their own unique vibrational signature and therefore are identifiable as separate individuals, they are both aligned with the energy of the same ray. That is the ray of teacher. DK's role is not dissimilar to Kuthumi, but his teaching takes on a different "feel."

It is the feeling of a young, wise and witty soul who has fun with his task. He's often found to be cracking jokes, with an uncanny ability to bring the listener to a point of letting go of their old stodgy beliefs that so often block enlightenment. He presents a new way of integrating a sometimes difficult or hidden aspect of human understanding and in the process delights not only the soul but also the funny bone.

As so many of the guides and masters often do, DK shares with people his delight in opening up minds and hearts to insights that are at once deep and ironic. His humor is his hallmark. "How could the truth of the universe be any other way?" he once remarked to me. Yes indeed, I thought, if there is no joy in it, why would anyone want to go there?

His and Kuthumi's energies are both of "a blue-green harmony," he says, "closely associated and connected with the essence of Earth." In this context, both he and Kuthumi work with the same aspects of the plan for Earth's evolution and are clear empaths, helping others to feel their own harmony with Earth and for Earth's advancements in her own development toward the Light. I have often wondered if my being an empath also draws me to love the interaction with these two so much. I once asked DK what he meant by the word *empath*. He responded as follows:

"For us in pure spirit form, it is easy to feel the love, energy and essence of another being, whether human, animal, plant, or elemental (Earth) essence. When we teach those still in physical form on the Earth, those who are currently perceiving separation, we allow them to connect with our energy in such a way as to allow them to experience *through us* the call to oneness. It is in this state of oneness, so easy in spirit, that you can join in empathetic union with others. It is as if we allow our boundaries to become soft and permeable to others so they can join with us in this endeavor."

I found his explanation to be quite similar to what I experience when I channel the masters.

DK's personality is very gay. I mean this not in the contemporary sense of being homosexual but in the old fashioned meaning of the word, light, happy, carefree and easy going—a perfect example of the path of effortlessness we are all being shown. He embodies the essence of love in such a way as to show the joy of the human spirit to us in unique ways of laughter, bliss, and total harmony. His essence is light, airy, but also clear and penetrating. In fact, it is because it is so light that it can penetrate almost any darkness with humor or with wisdom.

For some reason, I sometimes view DK as a younger Kuthumi who is still having fun playing and can't be bothered with anything too serious. Still, his wisdom is as profound as any master, which you will see when you read the channeling below. When asked about the transition the Earth is about to go through, he had the following to say in February of 1999:

"It is time now to go through the looking glass and discover what Alice did. She saw a myriad of human forms all delightful and joyful. She kissed the rabbit with her heart and spirit and embraced the joy of learning so freely that she put away all her old forms of enlightenment to learn a new technique of love. In integrating the loving and magical ways of the rabbit hole, she saw *through* the looking glass to penetrate to the knowledge base of the universe and find a new way of seeing. It is the way of joy.

"It is the way of going about life joyfully and playfully without preconceptions or foolish adult notions of what life is or should be all about. Imagine if she saw only what she thought she would see. She would have missed the Cheshire Cat, the magic mushrooms, the queen, and all the rest.

"The entire universe of thought is waiting for you to integrate it but only if you can let go of what you expect it to be and what it has been for you in the past. Only then can you be prepared to open up to the new awareness of the Crystal City, the Emerald City of the New Earth, and the juxtaposition of these two.

"These two are joined only in divine thought. The one stands upon the other awaiting your survey of them. The Crystal City exists in thought only, the pure thought of divine mind. It is the divine mind that goes beyond thought of third dimension intellect. The escape from unceasing thought, in the traditional sense, which you have all been awaiting, is in divine mind. It is the escape from duality, which is also the escape from illusion. This is what Alice found.

"She found all she had to do was think something into being. This is not third dimension; it is divine mind. Divine mind exists within the causal body of the Earth. By opening up to the divine mind, you manifest it within the causal body of the Earth's sphere. You and the Earth are doing this together so that the true plan of the New Earth and the New Universe is unfolding even now.

"Now is the time for you to make choices from your dreams, not from you old reality of what is possible. For in divine mind, the source of creation is all-possible. In your dreams is all possible, too. But, let us return to Alice.

"It could be said that Alice's trip through the looking glass is a journey into the center of one's soul. In this journey, no limitation is known or even conceived of. This is why all is possible; limitation does not exist in your soul. The timeless you has no boundaries. It is the realm of the superconscious, the realm of oneness with divine mind. Please do not mistake here that your intellect can take you to divine mind. Only if you become like Alice and believe in miracles can you do this!

" Eternity exists in the realm of the superconscious. But, of course, you must be willing to leave behind your old thoughts and ideas of what reality is to go there. You must become willing to let go of who you think you are, that is to say, your personality. If this seems too confusing simply let go and dive into the rabbit hole!

"With faith you can do this. But faith only brings you to brink. It is the divine plan that guides you to the edge—the edge of your own consciousness—and the Divine Mind within that urges you to jump! And jump you will if you are to see the new reality and enter into the New Earth. Even your old wise teachings tell you this: "There will be a new heaven (the New Universe) and a *New Earth."* Your new playground! Is this not fun and exciting? Of course it is. It is what you have all been awaiting, your new joy. But you cannot create it yourself as you are so used to *thinking* about. You must receive it instead.

"This is where so many of you run into trouble. You have your faith, and you are separate from it. You *believe* but you do not receive! For receiving is a thing unto itself, separate and distinct from believing. To receive, you must let go of believing. Does this mean you must surrender your faith?

"'Huh!' many of you say. 'To have the bounty of my faith, I must let go of my faith? That does not make sense.' Indeed it does not...in the third dimension, that is. But, you are no longer in third dimension when you reach this point. This is exactly what I am talking about. Let go of your non-expansive, limited, linear mind and receive. Receive from the heart and soul of you. You must see *through* the mind, not with it.

"The point is, when you let go of the old way of doing things, your *pre-conception* of how things are done, you let go of the Old World, the old Earth, and enter into the new! You go down the rabbit hole where the old rules of order do not apply. That is why you must dream your dreams and let yourself own them. Live them for good, for eternity! Only then will you thrive in your new identity as Master of the Universe, co-creator of All That Is. Isn't that secretly the way you want it to be anyway? A universe ruled by you; ruled by love. In the secret desire of your heart, hidden way down under all the pain and confusion, is a desire to be in your own little world where everyone loves and cherishes you. Welcome to the New Earth! Come greet your new friends here, too. They share your story. They share your dream. Welcome home.

"Only in Divine Mind—where you can go beyond faith, beyond reason, to have faith—is this possible. Only here is this new reality your new reality of *choice*. In truth, this has always been here waiting for you.

"Choose then to love and choose to dream your dreams of love. For in that loving universe you are the center—not the center as ego knows it, a cold and heartless center of a joyless ego existence, but the center of love as only God knows it. And you *are It*!"

*   *   *

In another channeling I did in 1999, Djwal Khul talks about healing and the Earth. In his usual inimitable manner, he challenges us to take ourselves less seriously:

"Greetings wise Masters. Today, let us talk about the Earth and how all plants, animals and energies work together for the common good of everyone.

"First though, let us speak of meditation, what it truly is and how you can organize your efforts to achieve the results you desire. It is necessary for you to have a basic understanding of the flow of life within you and without you—which is what you tap into during meditation—if you are to understand about the birds and the bees. As you will soon see, the birds and bees have a greater understanding of you than you do of them. Do not whet your appetite, however, if you are thinking about the "bird and bees" as you did when you were a teenager. There is truly a difference!

"Many have asked how it is possible to connect with a specific spirit guide or a master in the etheric. It is not just a matter of connecting with one single energy. In the etheric, many of the higher dimension guides and masters take their being from the fabric of love itself and are not limited to only one realm, as you are limited to the third dimension. Their being, indeed their growth as beings, is involved with taking small filaments of energy from each place in the higher vibrations and combining them to form a new richness of being and experience, like weaving many different threads into a beautiful tapestry. Since the identity of *being* in the upper realms comes from love itself, that love may originate from many different places at once. When you open yourself to this you will often experience new sensations.

"To connect with the essence of a particular master, you must be open to the *flow* of love instead of being open to a fixed or specific being with a name. You must float with this and allow your essence to co-mingle with theirs. It is a very different feeling than just a feeling of being in your body. It is not strictly a third-dimensional experience; it is yet intangible for you.

Since you are moving into the realm of many intangibles there will be a range of senses to which you will gradually become acclimated. Simply be open to *all* experiences without judgment and without expectation. Then you will be ready to learn many new things.

"Most of you are only open to a small range of experiences beyond the third dimension. As you all travel the ascension path toward greater light, you will find much diversity. Indeed you will find much diversity within yourself when you allow your concept of who you are to expand. You are beings of variation and change. Is it not true that you are a different person than you were a year ago? A month ago? A day ago? Begin to see yourself in this way: a being of flow and diversity, a being who could, if it chose to, fit into a tiny mushroom on the ground and experience life from the ground up. That is simply life *in combination of form* with another.

"Do not suppose that by *eating the mushroom* you could experience the same thing however! The mushroom would, but you would not! Many of you who have experienced various Earth lifetimes did this, but it did not work as well as you would have liked. Trust our experience and try this in the garden of your mind, not in your dining room.

"So you see, change is part of the mechanism of how you, too, derive your being from the fabric of All That Is, taking from it your substance anew each day. Did you suppose the Masters from whom you sought wisdom did not change from day to day as well? That would mean they never grew, and that is foolishness. They are not above you as many of you suppose. They are alongside you, growing with you in the process known as eternal enlightenment. It is a walk of joy where we all grow together. Indeed are we not one?

"Many of the things those of you ask about come from the intellect, and you know you must now learn to ponder things on a different wavelength. You must come to a place of allowing your heart to separate from your intellect for the time being. Meditation is essentially a thoughtless place. A place of not doing, but being. You must also allow it to become of place of feeling. It is a rich source of feelings on many levels.

"Meditation is not an exercise of going blank in your mind and emotions. It is a place of perception. A place where your feelings take flight and help you expand into the eternal. If you cannot accept the emotions you experience in meditation, you are not ready for it.

"Consider for example the concept of linear time and being able to expand or contract time for your own purposes or your own pleasure! To do this you must reach a place where you ponder this concept completely on a feeling level. Otherwise the brain will become water-logged with thought and twist itself into a miasma of confusion trying to comprehend what it was not designed to understand.

"Using your intuition first allow at least one aspect of this new concept to be sparked into light. Then follow that spark with no thought, but with feeling, intuitive feeling, to the next feeling or idea and allow your conscious mind to be *led*. The result will be an expansion of awareness your brain could not conceive of on its own. This is but one example. There are countless other examples and concepts awaiting your exploration.

"This exercise will bring into being for you a new faculty of sense: You receive (on a feeling level), expand into awareness, stay open to receive, expand into awareness again, and so on. It is simply a function of *receiving* the awareness. It is understanding in a new way. It may not make sense, but it does work. Be careful not to fall into analyzing or judging the new information. This will take you out of receiving and will stop the expansion.

"The expansion of awareness you experience is actually the expansion into a relationship with many other beings who hold knowledge and truth within themselves. They hold their divine minds open to you, their beings are always ready to receive you in your quest for a greater understanding of who you are. In this way, you receive greater light and knowledge and they receive communion with you. It matters not if you are consciously aware of the new beings you encounter in any given meditation. The connection is made, nonetheless.

"In fact, you travel great distances when you combine your energies in such a way. In our dimension, thoughts are things and they are how you travel. You travel great distances with your thoughts. Third-dimensional travel is understood as the illusion of travel. You drag your physical body around the globe, sometimes arriving back at your place of embarkation without having learned anything new at all! Sometimes we watch you do this for our own amusement. You have no idea how entertaining it can be.

"In our realm, your thoughts *physically* take you to new places. Indeed, this is how many masters on the Earth were able to travel around the planet without dragging their bodies on boats, mules, or walking. They were able to let their thoughts flow and intermingle with their feelings. With feelings as transportation, they traveled about. You on Earth plane call this *teleporting*. When you get very good at traveling with your spirit in meditation, you will then be ready to learn how to take your body with you. But that is food for later thoughts."

During group, someone in the audience asked DK, "Would the thought of desiring information take me to the particular master who could teach, I mean, share, this information with me?"

DK responds, "An excellent question, but no, I'm afraid not. You see, this is not something you use your *desire* to do. Desire is of the third plane. Desire is a part of your humanness. It is associated with cause and effect. But thought travel in our dimensions is not associated with desire in the same way that you desire a thing in third dimension. When you desire something in third dimension, you are aware of something you lack. When you desire something in our realm, you are aware that you already contain this knowledge by being part of the oneness of All That Is.

"When you accept you are part of the oneness that is God you simply go to the place within yourself where the needed knowledge is stored. Though it is seemingly within another being, it is still a part of who you are. It is not something you are separate from. Let us use the analogy of being in a large house with a vast library. You desire knowledge that is contained in one of your books. So without feeling any absence of what you seek, you go to the shelf on which the book rests and make this knowledge your own. Nothing has been taken from the book it does not still have and yet you now know what you were looking for. You have become one with the knowledge.

"When you begin to feel your connection to all other life, and life forms, to all other knowledge and teachings, you will begin to grasp what I am talking about. Remember, it is not the intellect that directs your actions or your thoughts, but the feelings and intuition. They are contained in the heart and the body. Allow your mind only to be sparked with curiosity, then let your heart go wandering for new insights and awareness. Your heart is the driver, your intuition is the vehicle, and your intellect is the passenger.

"So when you desire information or connection with guides or masters, you must begin not from a feeling of lack but from your center of peace, knowing that all is one and that you already contain that which you seek. In this you must trust yourself; there is no other way to succeed. In this way success is not something you achieve but something you already contain, too. Ponder these things I have spoken to you, but please be gentle with yourselves and laugh much in the process. You are astonishing beings, filled with joy and play. Please partake of this joy often. You will be amazed at how much you will learn by simply playing and being in joy."

As always after channeling Djwal Khul, I return to my body fully feeling like I have just had a good romp in the hay with a trusted and fun-filled friend who is ready for anything. Try a trip down the rabbit hole yourself sometime with DK. It is worth a ride.

DK then went on to talk about Earth and our connection with her. He seems to delight in delving into matters most elemental. The following comes from the same session:

"Now let us speak of your connection to Earth and all her creation. Many of you, in your wisdom, are returning to the old ways of healing the Earth and to the old ways of honoring her as a sentient being, interacting with her as an equal. In truth, she is a being of great magnitude and beauty. If you could only see how even now she nurtures your species with steadfast patience, you would all at once come to understand unconditional love.

"It is gradually becoming known by many how beneficial it is to use natural means to encourage the plants to grow and yield their fruits. Instead of forcing the growth of life in plants and animals, nurture that life, treasure it that it would be free to choose to benefit you and your body by giving its life freely. To force a plant to grow with chemicals and poison Earth in the process is like forcing a lover to give up his or her blessing to you without asking what *they* want.

"The Earth *is* your lover. Entreat her not with threats and abuse, for she has much to give you of her own free accord with joy and gentleness. Many of the plants here to bless you now shrink from your touch fearing harshness. That is why many of your wild plants still carry the ability to nourish and heal while your domesticated plants do not. The wild ones, unaccustomed to the harshness of your forced labors, still carry a great love for all humans. Many of the wild plants are admired for their tenacity, some growing in harsh or extreme conditions. Indeed, these ones are valued for their very rarity.

"When plants are admired in this way, it is no different than smiling at a child who then comes lovingly into your arms giving love freely. Begin entertaining the idea of creating *relationships* with all living things and accepting them as sentient. They are indeed sensitive and conscious. It is not just their leaves and tendrils that have awareness but their spirit as well. Their spirits support the physical form as yours does. They are in union with higher dimensions at all times. They are in union with Earth and her plan for the enlightenment of all. If you are quiet enough, you can hear this plan in your own heart.

"Knowing this, how can you doubt that they know their purpose? Indeed, how can you think you know how they should grow better than they do? "Though you do not retain a conscious memory or awareness of your union with the higher dimensions, they do. You can learn from them. They remind you of your connections to higher dimensions and to the divine plan of Earth so that you can draw from them the energy and sustenance needed to heal your physical bodies and stay in alignment with truth. The healing of your minds and spirits is also remedied by these your fellow beings of Earth.

"Sometimes a plant wishing to be enveloped into a new form of life is eaten and its life force is absorbed into your body. There is now a communion of your life and the plant. This communion state is shared far more often that you would guess. The plant gives its life to you and, in turn, it receives a new experience of life in the richness of diversity. Thus, it is an experience of give and take with gratitude on all parts. Take joy in this, and, by all means, give gratitude for what you have received. Do this not in the form of prayers that have become stale like old bread but in sharing joy while living.

"Healing in the natural way is not to wait for the body to start to die or become diseased. As your body becomes aware of a cell in an organ that is tired and wishes to depart—dissolving itself once again into the flow of life and All That Is—it is natural for your body to bring in nourishment for the reproduction of that single cell. In this way the body stays vital, alive and well and always maintaining itself in the flow.

"What you call your body is not a static physical form but a community of many lives—cells that come and go with their own free will. It is a cooperation of spirits and of life, a reservoir of knowledge that is being shared together and with you. It is an uncommonly sympathetic arrangement that allows for the steady continuation of your consciousness in physical form. The life of your consciousness is so pure and so intense it can not be held in a dead form, but only in cooperation of a community of living cells, living beings, all communing with one another in peaceful coexistence.

"Let the health of your body be determined by the consensus of the community of beings that you are. Always honoring each of those beings with free choice, with the same dignity and respect you honor yourself.

Life of those beings on Earth is not separate but exists as a continuum of life in all things. The richness of that life is there for you to enjoy. Indeed, even physical pleasures are joys experienced by many cells at once. When you feel great pleasure, it is because there is great joy and bliss felt by the community of your cells together in celebration.

"It is meant that your entire body should celebrate all at once. That is why you are here. That is why they are here. To join in conscious contact with living divine awareness of Self.

"It is the conscious, living, divine awareness of Self that I embody most effortlessly and perfectly. It is why I carry such youthfulness. It is why when you align with my energy all of your cells are grateful. They have some measure of awareness of what I contain and represent. Many of you are coming to understand this as well. It does not matter if all of this is done on a conscious level. Your cells, even your brain cells, feel the knowledge that you are honoring them as living beings with free choice in the highest regard.

"If this is all too much for you right now, begin with a feeling of awe at how much your "body" contains. Let respect then flow from that awe, and you will have love for all of yourself. When the respect then deepens to a loving regard, you will have communication with your cells. You will be amazed at what they have to show you about yourself. The cells of your body will be delighted to send you conscious knowledge of how much they love you as well.

"When the loving relationship is established in conscious form, your body will experience an accelerated rate of healing. All of your cells will be cheering. All of them will be filling with love. Those cells that do not wish to join in the celebration, for whatever reason, will then leave your body. New cells will replace them, keeping your body ever vital.

"Yet, even in your awareness of this there will always be a great mystery at how and why this happens. It is not important you understand the depth of the mystery. It is only important that you have a respect and reverence for it. In this way, you are constantly sending loving attention to each of the cells of the community of your body. In this loving gratitude and connection there is a sense of wholeness. When that wholeness is complete, the communion is then intact for all. Then you will experience perfect, youthful, vital health.

"When one organ of your body is ailing, go to that place and ask the cells why they are not in celebration and what they require of you. If you cannot give them what they need, tell them they are free to move on because there are those cells that wish to celebrate in their stead. This does not mean that you are saying, "I cast you out." It simply honors their free choice. Since you are the choir director of the body, you are asking everyone to sing in harmony. It is not an unreasonable request.

"When you honor your cells with the awe and respect they deserve, you are then capable of honoring your own free choice with the same respect. Since you are the director and you honor all cells equally, they will honor you by conforming to joy or by leaving all others to celebrate together. It is the simplest of things to create healing for yourself in this way. You are not pushing aside anyone in fear or in anger.

" your bodies and your planet will come to the same arrangement, changing by the freely chosen departure of those who live in fear. Those cells in the community not celebrating and choosing to remain in fear will leave. That is why if you visualize your body filling with light and all of your cells celebrating health and vitality. Those cells choosing darkness will shrink from the light and leave you. Light—indeed love—is the true healer.

"When you give in to fear of disease, you give your power to those cells not singing in the joyful harmony of your body. It is like telling them they can now become the directors of your body. Stay firm and in clear knowledge that you are a better choir director because you have a more clear perspective than they do. Honor your knowing the truth of vital health. When you hold this knowledge brightly within for all cells to see, they will respond to that call. Indeed, vital health is the highest truth held for the community of cells that are learning their own wisdom by being a part of your body.

"They come to learn this knowledge, for this knowledge is love. When they stay in a state of knowing this truth, they stay in bliss and are able to receive love. So those cells still in fear, choosing not to love, are honored because of free choice. But because love is a higher vibration, they will seek lower forms of consciousness.

"Even the air you breathe contains energies of atoms that desire communion with you. For even the air is alive. It is the same with everything you take into your body: sunlight, plants, minerals, water. All of these things then join you in your community. Even the plants who so gratefully receive your acceptance of them as equals and masters will sometimes choose to join with you and become a part of your body to experience that form of bliss before returning once again to the Earth.

"Many energies, beings, do not choose just one form in which to exist. They may choose to travel throughout many forms in the Earth. Sometimes air. Sometimes earth. Sometimes water. The continuum of experience is enjoyable to them.

"In the higher realms, we have often been asked about the eating of animals. This is a weighty matter. Please be aware that most of you now eating animals give little thought to what the animals want. Are they not also exquisite beings of free choice as you are? I say this to instill no guilt but to inform you that there is a better way.

When you desire to take sustenance in the form of animal flesh, go to the spirit of the animal asking permission. Commune with that animal and if given acceptance of taking this animal's life, give wholesome gratitude to the animal concerned. Many animals are glad to be of service in this way and to experience becoming a part of your body in the way plants do. All is one and always will be. Please be kind enough to ask for permission first though, and do not take until you can feel a gift being given to you.

"We have discoursed quite enough for now. Is your understanding complete enough to allow you to give your body more vitality, indeed, more free choice with direction? The direction of joy in celebration of life and of health. You can now begin to experience more fully who you are as a living breathing community of beings in which your spirit is the director and guide.

"We are grateful for your attention and interest, and as always, to be of service to you. Let the God of your being find joy and bliss in celebration of life. May we be as one in this. God in one. One in all. Go in peace and be as one, all you who seek enlightenment."

Chapter 10

El Morya and the Garden of Being

Channeling El Morya gives me the feeling I am in the midst of a grand ongoing celebration, a feast, a tribute to everything that is great in the universe. It's as if he draws to his corner of the ethers all those who love a good party and want to join in the merry making. His laughter is quick and so too his decisiveness. He will go a long way to help you connect with him, but if you lie to yourself or try to deceive others, he will be quick to point that out to you. He will always expose your dishonesty but then hold your hand while you weep about any regret or mistakes made. He knows all too well what it is to be human. Some say he was King Arthur when in the physical. As with the other masters I channel, this does not concern me as much as who he is now and how he communicates his love to others.

El Morya is intense rather than soft-spoken, and he can easily be mistaken for being brusque, but he is not. It is simply that his tenderness is only exposed when needed. It's as if he immediately extends his hand to you looking you straight in the eyes accepting you as his equal and expects you will do the same. Though you may look in the mirror and see a medley of fears and insecurities, El Morya sees only another master and speaks to you thusly. Your fears are as nothing to him. He fairly commands you to hold your head up. He challenges you to accept your power and step up to his level.

El Morya's earthiness fuels his passion of all things physical. Though he is in spirit form, I think he is the guide most able to help others with issues of their physical senses. His heartiness, when I act as his vessel, allows me to feel a connection with the Earth I do not often come close to experiencing with the other masters except, of course, the Council of Elders. Though etheric in nature, he retains a robustness of spirit I feel in my own body when he joins with me. Even though he is not material in form, he belies the distinction of etheric master by being ardent, full of genuine emotional expression and loving to a fault. In short, El Morya is ready for anything we in the Earth pose to him as long as it involves allowing him to teach love and have a good time in the process. He will hold no court for undue self-pity.

Many people, most notably women, are drawn to El Morya for his passion and verve, the masculine warrior and lover of old. This is not so with me. Of El Morya's many characteristics, I think it is his sense of justice I admire most. True, his passion is limitless, but his sense of honor carries a depth of thoughtfulness unequaled by others as he reaches out to all who hold out hope of receiving grace and equality in spirit. It is this that touches me most deeply. Perhaps if he did live a life as King Arthur, he vowed to treat everyone equally, and in spirit, he remains true to that oath.

A sovereign if ever there was one, El Morya is our divine equal, showing us that we too can drink from the cup of life. Of fairness and virtue he has said, "True justice is justice of the soul. A just God includes all and leaves out no one. For whomsoever is divine, will see the divinity in everyone and in everything else. When all this is done, we shall see that all is one." He is a poet as well.

I first met El Morya before I actually began my career as a channel. It was not until years later that I recognized him as the one who came to me so early on. During the period when I was first learning how to offer information and healing to others, I often found myself getting together with my friend, Lilly, for some informal morning meditations. It helped us stay focused on our goals of being connected in spirit with our guides. On this particular morning we were just finishing up at her house, chatting over a cup of tea.

Lilly's neighbor Debbie came over to visit. She was feeling lots of stress from a number of difficult situations in her life and came seeking some support and help. She had an assortment of body ailments that left her low on physical energy and was also experiencing tension over some legal problems her husband was having. She wasn't sure what to ask and didn't even know how to approach the many different stresses in her life to find release and gain a measure of inner peace.

Lilly and I had already set up her healing/massage table that morning before we meditated, though, at the time we didn't know why. Upon Debbie's arrival, it became clear that all was being divinely guided. We invited Debbie to lay down on the table as we prepared to run some energy for her. My friend Lilly had been encouraging me for weeks to begin using the psychic gifts I was finding I had, to benefit others. It was with her gracious, loving and supportive insistence I found the courage to step up to the table and connect with Debbie. As I approached her, I felt a quickening within me, as if a part of me was coming to life.

As I stood at the head of the table, with Lilly at Debbie's feet, I felt a rush of energy begin flooding into my body from the ground up. I could feel my feet tingle and a flood of intense vitality rose up into my legs and thighs. I thought for a moment I would lift right off the ground and fly! It was as exhilarating as it was exciting, and I was dazzled. I continued to allow the energy inside me to build up. I had no idea what to expect next, so I relaxed into the moment. Soon I felt the energy rise up to my throat, and I felt compelled to speak. The words formed themselves as I simply let them flow out of me. I was about to experience for the first time the beauty of El Morya in the Garden. He has taken several people into this Garden through me since then, and the words he speaks are as beautiful and flowing as that first time with Debbie:

"Join me my lovely friend, for a walk in the Garden of Being. Set aside all your troubles and having nothing more to do than enjoy the beautiful flowers, relax. Breathe deeply of life itself and be renewed. Let us walk past the hedges and the beautiful leaves of green. Drink in the air of gratitude for the sunshine in your life, and relax deeply with me by your side. Take my arm and let me lead you. Soon we come to the little garden within the garden, for there are many of these within your beautiful essence. We come now to the garden of delights.

"There are many things in this land of delight. All things radiate the bliss of oneness. In this bliss is the togetherness you may feel you have lost. It is the space in your heart you struggle to reclaim. The Garden is within your heart, but it is within my heart, too. In this we are the same. We hold this space together and share in its beauty. You are not alone in the Garden. It is not that we are exactly alike, but I am with you and we see each other in mutual divinity. As we walk together, we are one and we know the bliss of eternal beings in love."

I couldn't believe what words were coming out of my own mouth! Never before had I let go so completely to let the flow of information and blessing from spirit continue on and on. What amazed me most was the effortlessness of it all. I knew these words were not coming from my own intellect. It was rather that I heard them the instant they were spoken by my own mouth. I felt so blessed to be participating in this. It was the most humbling experience I'd had in my life. It was also strangely uplifting at the same instant. It fit exactly a definition for humility I'd heard years before from a friend. He said, "Humility is knowing your place and taking it." Such simplicity and grace and I was in the thick of it. If this was what channeling held for me, I was ready for it.

I looked down at Debbie. Her body was no longer stiff and rigid, she had relaxed almost as soon as the first few words were being spoken. I knew without a doubt this had been divinely orchestrated for us all—for me, to dive into the world of psychic work, for Debbie to receive healing and perhaps for Lilly to be an integral part of divine synchronicity at work. Lilly was elated. It was what she had been telling me about all along. What I could experience by simply letting it happen amazed me. It seemed to amaze her, too. Who I now know was then El Morya, continued on:

"Do not struggle to feel my presence, for I am here as always. But feel your own being here in the Garden. Feel your own heart space and then you will know truly I am with you as always and cannot leave you. But do not love me more than yourself; if you do, your heart will be lonely for it will not have you, and you are more important than I am. When you make me more important than you are, then indeed you are alone. It is not the loss of others' love that you miss so dearly; it is the loss of your own love for yourself that causes you pain. So walk with me still, and I will lead you into this love.

"As we continue to walk together in spirit, see the images in the Garden that represents all aspects of your own nature: loving, peaceful, serene, and joyful, playful as the sunflowers in the wind when they bend their heavy heads laden with the oil of bliss. Dipping down to entice other creatures to come drink of the oil of oneness.

"There is a stream in the Garden just this side of the sunny palms. How like you to place a warm area for others to rest and find warmth. How like you to hold truths out in the sunshine so they are easily reached and not toiled for. In the effortless of your divine love for others, you send tendrils of your heart to encircle the lonely ones who have yet to find their way into the Garden, gently gathering other souls, drawing them in. Not because they have no choice but because the fragrances of spirit, the flowers of nurturing urge them to receive.

"The tree of my love with its knowledge of self-love is waiting to give you a branch to plant for yourself so that you may have your own tree to become your source. The loveliness of your tree is equal to that of every other tree in the forest in the Garden of Being. You will never want for anything, for all will be within your reach. How is your tree growing? Does it need water, or a little pruning? Being the diving gardener is a skill that takes time to develop. But in the Garden of Being there is all the time in the world.

"No bird sings as sweetly as when you are laughing. So great is our welcoming of you into the Garden, we entreat you to bring your laughter so we can all enjoy the sound. We await your touch in spirit as you reach out to fulfill *your* destiny by being one with us. The Garden of Your Being is a sacred place where you can experience direct communion with your own divine essence, your higher-self, in its purest form. Please walk there with me often, and I will share my love with you."

As I finished speaking the words given to me, I noticed the surge of energy was gone. I was left with a feeling of deep peace and satisfaction, a reverence for what had just happened. I knew without a doubt that it did not come from me, but from the joining of the three of us with those assisting us in spirit. I knew I had just witnessed something that was sure to happen over and over again if I was willing to allow it.

At the end of the experience, Debbie arose from the table. Much of her physical stiffness and soreness was gone. Her face was the picture of serenity and peace. She had let go of her fear about how the stressful events in her life were going to unfold. It wasn't that all her problems were gone but as she explained it, her mind was now at rest and her heart no longer felt alone. She told me that much of her physical strength had returned too. When the mind is at rest, the body is relieved of its burden.

I have watched the masters guide many people through different blissful and joyful experiences but the Garden of Being remains my favorite. I first encountered it at the very birth of my career as a channel and psychic. I don't think Debbie was ever quite the same; I know I wasn't.

In other channelings much later in my life, I have often asked El Morya about instruction or information on entering the Garden. He has given me the following advice. It is El Morya who speaks:

A Prelude to the Garden

"When you desire to enter your own Garden of Being, you must let go of your old ideas about who you are. You see, my lovely ones, you are not who you think you are. You are more divine, more beautiful than even your own mind can fathom. You must yield to this. Yield to the new you, the beautiful you that I see in your own eyes. Yield to the fabric of a changing reality that worships you as God. In the Garden it is so. The Garden itself worships you. It is a mirror for you own beauty. Prepare yourself to know this.

"When you are in the Garden, you will see it is true. Before entering you must become willing to worship yourself. If you cannot, you will have trouble believing what is shown to you. You will trick yourself into believing that it is a kind compliment I give and not the truth as I see it. This is a worthless belief; it is a lie. I do not patronize you or wish to do so. I do not flatter; I speak only the truth. When I look at you I see only beauty. You must come to believe this is the purest of truths. Only then will you come to release your old picture of self. Self in the Garden is God. It has always been so. Walk with me now."

In subsequent channelings, El Morya offered still more information on the Garden of Being.

"The Garden of Being is the place you go to find communion with your essence, your higher-self. When you first interact with this space, it is hard to delineate because it is a purely spiritual realm and hard to translate into a third-dimensional understanding. We have spoken briefly beforehand about allowing your thoughts and feelings to be drawn up into the higher realms so you can experience firsthand these new things.

" I am well acquainted with much magical energy in the Garden of Being, and I so I spend much time here greeting souls who come in to experience communion with their essence. I walk with many who are in the Garden, perceiving and enjoying the delights with them. I find much joy and gratitude in being with others in this place. As you go to this place often, you may find there are many of us with you in spirit. As you become more acquainted with this space of the spirit, we become more easy to recognize and easier for you to see as your equals.

"There are many of us here to greet you and you may find yourself having conversations with us there. Do not be dismayed to find that as you commune here you become accustomed to greeting us as equals as a matter of course. This is the way it is in the Garden. All of us are equal and all of us are one, enjoying bliss together.

"Some of you will first experience simply a lessening of interaction with your mind as it quiets itself and allows you to roam the ethers without its interruptions. There may also be a growing feeling of peacefulness and an inner knowing that all is well. This is good. It is a good start. In your first experiences in the garden, you may find yourselves much distracted with the bliss, too. Enjoy this aspect for as long as you please, and when you are ready to have conversations, we will be there. We will wait for you and try not to distract you from your enjoyment!

"Also in the garden you may perceive remembrances from past lifetimes. They will usually relate to your present lifetime in some way or another to allow you to learn a lesson that is pertinent for you at this time. Do not struggle with the learning, just relax and watch the scene unfold for you before your eyes. Allow the messages and images to play across your consciousness without trying to analyze or understand them.

Analyzing will draw you out of the Garden and back into your thinking mind, your intellect. Relax and be at peace.

"You may find some frustration at first with only half clear images appearing, but do not try to make more images come or fill in what you would consider missing details. This too will draw you back to your intellect. More will come with practice, but this is part of the effortlessness of the experience and it is provided for you as a gift.

"As you move into the effortless space, simply enjoy what you feel and take a hand when it is offered. I, or perhaps another, will commune with you. You will feel my energy and that of others as you relax into the Garden. You may feel or see your guides, other beings who have come to experience their own essence, or other teachers such as myself. Gradually, you will be able to detect the subtle nuances between yourself and the others who are there.

"This will be true for experiencing others' presence here too. Feel your own peace and bliss before you go searching for others to join in the bliss with you. It is a simple thing to take one piece at a time. Have patience, my loved ones, and you will find your joy sooner than later, for rushing headlong into these experiences without taking time to discern them and their fine points will cause unwanted delays.

"When you approach the concept of oneness, you must first learn it is not so important that you become one with a being called God than it is that you become one with your own divine self. First oneness with Self, then oneness with others constitutes oneness with God. The oneness of all individuals together in love is what you call God. When you feel a oneness with even one other person, it is a small layer of oneness with God.

"The task of oneness with God is not so huge as it might seem. It is instead very close to your own center. You do not need to go great distances to find this. You probably are already involved in the process of self-acceptance.

"The more you relax and allow the natural processes to do their job without your ego or intellect trying to help them, the more you will see it is a fluid thing. Indeed, you only need to watch as if from a distance and see the beauty of how it manifests and unfolds for you.

"The body will breathe fluidity and peacefully on its own if you do not consciously think about how to draw your breath in and out. If you do decide to think about breathing, it most assuredly interferes with this natural function. If you look also at walking and breathing and try to do these two things consciously, your coordination will be all askew, will it not? So relax I say, and allow your higher self to go about its business and be at peace.

"When you allow the higher-self to guide your path, soon everything you do is with divine acknowledgment of who you are. This bathes you in a state of joy. Have joy, and live effortlessly, as you will do when you allow the higher-self to guide you. Let go and return to the childlike innocence you have in the Garden, and you will soon see it becomes automatic for you to stay there. I await a joyful encounter with your beautiful essence. I see it as a flower even now, slowly opening to show the world its profound beauty."

El Morya's first encounter with me was without any fanfare to announce his regal presence. I didn't even know until years later when I heard him speak of the Garden again that it was he I channeled that day. It is like him to do things this way. It is like that with all the masters. They do not need nor desire accolade for themselves; they serve in humility wanting only for us to receive love, joy and healing. I never quite get accustomed to this. The world I live in, the world we all live in, seeks acclaim and honor. It is only when we yield to the grace of God that we are worthy of receiving these things. Ironically, it is then that we have no more need of them.

El Morya remains at my side ready to act in behalf of others whenever there is need. His offer of a walk through the Garden is an open invitation for all who seek peace. Take him up on this offer, and see for yourself what tranquillity ensues. Bathe yourself in the light of your own divine presence. Come to know El Morya as a gentle and wise master that is ready and eager to guide you into the beauty of your own garden of being.

Chapter 11

Kuthumi: Friend across Time

It wasn't long before I was working with clients both on the phone and in person. As my clientele grew so did my ability to go into increasingly deeper spaces and into other dimensions to access information. I often found it was easier to go deeper with a client who was adept in making at least some connections with spirit on his/her own. This still holds true; when someone is able to receive from the other side it not only makes my job easier, I can also access deeper wisdom for them. It's almost as if their energy supports the entire process.

Even though northwestern Montana was relatively slow to open up to different areas of spirituality there were a few individuals living there who were as interested as I was in gaining new insights into a deeper connection with God. One of these people was an older woman whom I will call Janet. She was a pleasant woman with a beautiful spirit that sought more understanding of her spiritual path and yearned to know how she could be in alignment with it. She already had a connection with her spirit guides but called me now and again to pinpoint certain areas of growth she didn't understand. It was during one of my sessions with Janet that I met my own beloved master guide on the other side, Kuthumi.

I arrived at Janet's house, a small guest cottage in the backyard of a larger home. She had rented this place for a brief stay in the Kalispell area before moving on to other spiritual seeking in the southwest. As I walked into her home, I sensed an air of anticipation as our sessions were always filled with new insights sometimes for us both. Janet was also blessed with multiple gifts and we often traded information back and forth as it flowed. Sometimes the information was more easily gained by our combined energies focused on the area of concern.

On this particular day, we were seated at her kitchen table. It was raining outside and the rain made a peaceful tapping sound as it hit the windowpanes and fell on the roof. The sound of the rain and a fire in the wood stove made for a cozy environment that day and we both relaxed into an easy conversation about how we would tune-in and what information she needed. As Janet began sharing her thoughts with me and asking questions, I felt the energy in the room shift. This was usually my sign that a guide had entered my energy field and was ready to offer information. I relaxed and waited.

As I readied myself to receive information from the other side, I closed my eyes and was immediately enveloped in a vision of bright light. It was as if I was standing on another plane in the open air, surrounded by a misty atmosphere that was not of this world. I gazed ahead to see dark, somewhat hooded figure walking toward me in spirit, with a blue and white light streaming out from behind him. A sudden and utter calm came over me and I "knew" I was about to meet a new guide. Right after this, I was also filled with the knowledge of who he was. I said to Janet calmly, "Oh, Kuthumi is here." The words flowed out of my mouth as if I were reading a first grade primer. It was the easiest thing in the world to recognize his presence. However, it was the first time I could remember ever hearing the name or seeing his form in my mind. Some part of me knew without any doubt who he was and why he was here. What surprised me the most was how calmly I accepted all of this.

I do not always have perfect clarity in messages from the other side. Often their words come in bits and in snippets that I am only later able to piece together to gain a cohesive understanding. In this case, it was as clear as any message I have ever received and I never doubted who this was for a second. It was simply that I was recognizing an old friend and I knew it.

Kuthumi walked toward me in the vision and smiled. His smile was something I felt rather than saw. It radiated from his being to mine. It was as if his smile opened his heart to me and I felt such peace knowing he loved me. I knew I could not mistake the message he was about to give. I told Janet she was to receive a new guide herself. She confirmed this by saying she had been told earlier in the week that she would receive an angel into her life who would guide her. She'd been waiting for this but was still a bit amazed at the clear confirmation of it. Kuthumi continued to give her details of her path ahead, including how she would face some challenges in the coming weeks, but reassured her she would get through it and, in the end, would prevail.

The vision continued for some time, and as the information came to an end, so too did the vision in which I was enveloped. When Kuthumi left, I felt no sadness or loss; I knew he would come to me again. I felt only the deep peace I always felt after connecting with the other side.

I looked over at Janet and she too seemed relaxed and at peace. She was still a bit surprised at how quickly the confirmation of her new angel came. I was eager to see if she was worried about the upcoming challenges Kuthumi had told her about, but she was not. Her peace too seemed to allay all possible fears. It is often difficult to describe to people how the peace that flows from the other side is able to neutralize fear without promising a perfect life ahead. I think we all know life will continue to hold challenges for us all, but to know we are not alone and that we are helped is often enough to give us the courage to go on and face what lies ahead.

In fact, I am often surprised to see how many of my clients are willing, even eager, to receive information of this kind. I always wince internally as I am giving out information that seems to suggest a difficulty or challenge that is ahead. Most of the time people simply tell me they would much rather know what is ahead than be surprised with unexpected perils or growth issues and be caught unawares. It makes sense. Prepare for it and get through it rather than get hit with something blind. I guess I'd want to know that myself. I guess the ostrich approach doesn't work very well for anyone.

During the session that day, Janet also received details about other personal things, relationships that were ending and how her path of spirituality would broaden into her own work with people. It seemed Janet was to become more of a healer as well. I was forging a new relationship with Kuthumi simply by allowing him to communicate with Janet through me. I'd found an old friend I didn't remember I had. What I didn't yet know was just how good a friend he was and how much I would gain both personally and professionally from his presence in my life.

The vision I received of Kuthumi approaching me that day was so clear and striking I knew I wanted share it with others. The cover of this book is my vision of that day exactly the way I saw it. He suggested the image as a cover picture. In order to create the cover exactly as I saw him that day I described the image to my publications relations consultant and what he came up with on his first try is what you see. It mirrors so exactly the vision I received that I must believe it is Kuthumi himself who aided us both in creating it.

In the weeks and months that followed, my relationship with Kuthumi deepened and I used our connection to access more and more information for others. I started writing down his wisdom for others to read. It was as if there was no limit to what our combined energies could accomplish. As Kuthumi and I continued to work together I came to understand a sense of kindred spirits existed between us. A bond was forming (or was it just that I was "remembering" it?) that was unlike anything I had experienced with the other guides I spoke with or channeled. It was more like a oneness of spirit, a communion that enveloped us both when we connected. I was gratefully becoming more connected than ever before to the other side and the depth of my readings was strengthened. Though I still continued to channel the other masters, I came to know Kuthumi's presence was with me as a constant force, a great and loving force of peace.

I worked with Kuthumi in private sessions with clients but also began channeling him on a regular basis. I found his wisdom to be so great I couldn't help but want to share it with the world. My articles for the *Sedona Journal* began taking on a new level of authority, and I started hearing from readers more frequently about how the articles were helping them. I thought more and more of Kuthumi and I as a team. Sometimes I would channel him for groups and later transcribe the tapes into written articles. I also found I could take a partial message from a single client and together Kuthumi and I would expand it into a full article. Both methods seemed to work equally well.

Since the volume of material I have from Kuthumi is so great, I have tried to select a particularly profound text from him that seems to represent his teaching ability. One of the things I admire most about him is his ability to take deep spiritual concepts and communicate them in terms simple enough for anyone to understand. I think this is why people seem so touched by our work together.

I once received a message from him during a phone session with a client. As I was channeling him, I found my hand reaching for a piece of paper and pen. In a cryptic way he wrote "You are the apple of my eye," but in place of the words "apple" and "eye," he drew pictures of these things, like you would for a child. To be considered his protégé was enough for me, but to be compared with himself and likened to being his child was over the top. I was elated and in joy for days.

It's often hard to explain just how I receive messages from the guides. It is often an odd experience, one definitely not of this world. After channeling for several years, it's as if the veil between this world and the next is only partially there. I seem to live in two worlds at once with a foot in each. I often feel so many of the emotions the masters feel, even minute details of subtle understanding from their side of the veil that is difficult to communicate in words. I often struggle to express the great love they have for us, as well as the unlimited compassion for our struggles. One of the main reasons for my writing this book is to encourage people to connect for themselves so they too can feel the gentle intimacy I do when in communion with the unconditional love from the other side.

I would describe Kuthumi's teaching as wise, loving and clear. It is also profound, often funny in an almost highbrow way, and I find he has a very dry sense of humor. Not as joking-minded as Djwal Khul, Kuthumi has his own way with people, which is both engaging and very warm. Whether he is encouraging us to laugh at ourselves and our humanness, or laughing with us at the connection between dimensions and the corresponding confusion it often brings, his love is always at the heart of it. With him love is always the path and the goal.

After much deliberation, I decided to include a series of pieces published in 2000 and 2001 in the *Sedona Journal of Emergence*. I received many gracious and kind comments from readers about this series. It seems to address many of the concerns people have about healing, multidimensional living, and the ascension process to higher ways of living.

In addition, these sections carry an extremely high energy, one of Kuthumi's hallmarks. Feel the expert skill and love of this master, my best friend on the other side. See how he is able to condense even the most complex spiritual practices into understandable lessons, easy for most to grasp. Also, read these pieces with an ear to the vibration they carry and allow yourself the treat of "feeling the words" and absorbing the energy. It will take you on a ride to the higher dimensions of which he speaks. Enter into the world of magic and miracles and get ready to receive a miracle into your own life. Or as Kuthumi would say, "A miracle each and every day!" The dimension of love awaits.

Cellular Changes
Creates Multi-Dimensional Healing

Part I

"Greetings beloved ones. You are well in-tune with the many splendid changes occurring around the globe and the ascension of humankind is assured. There are still a few important ideas that will aid you in the process of becoming a clear and obvious picture of fifth-dimensional love here in third dimension. Let us begin with the process you are well familiar with called cellular re-programming, the changing of your bodies into light.

"What we will speak of today is photo-genetic change. It is the process of giving up sub-atomic particles within the body that hold fear and by virtue of this allowing more light to enter your physical body. This involves the rebuilding of your DNA. Photo-genetic change is the foundation of your ascension to a higher form of being. Indeed, you are already beings of great light but for most of you, this knowledge is hidden from you on an everyday level. I suggest you begin owning this knowledge not just on an intellectual or conscious level but on a very practical, everyday one, too.

"When you restructure your DNA by the process of photo-genetic change, as has always been in your power to do, you create new directions for the body to follow. The DNA is the directory of the body, each cell holding instructions that allow it to function at its highest physical and spiritual capacity. When your DNA is interacting with the fear that is held within the sub-atomic particles of each cell there is confusion about what course of action to follow. When you release your body from fear, clear direction is once again restored.

"Many of you hold fear about your own physical forms or fear you will be unwell and in pain. When you are able to believe and then accept that you create your own body of light and are ready to do so, you will no longer fear your present physical body. You see, you are in command of it and not it of you! You are not a victim of your body, of disease or of fear. You are free to choose your own emotional and physical experiences. The result of this is to experience bliss and freedom on an intimate, personal, existential level. Haven't you all had such experiences when, in a moment of joy and well being, you feel as if you are walking on air? This is the feeling of which I speak. Freedom to be in peace and in joy as *you* so choose. This is your birthright. Indeed, you are free to experience a state so elated that even your cells are in such unanimous bliss that you can almost float above the ground. Haven't all of you felt at least a brief moment of this? This is congruent self-love on multiple levels at once.

"The cells of your body each hold the memory of a variety of different experiences. This is the memory of your past, both this life and other lives. Some of these memories are distressing to you. When the body is in distress, ill health, or disease, these memories are coming to the surface. When you can recognize this. you can learn not to judge, run away from, or fear these memories. When these memories surface, you begin experiencing the inner environment of your cells that hold these experiences for you. Your cells hold these memories for you as a service. Often events that are too painful to be integrated at the moment they occur are stored by cells until the entire organism is ready to integrate the experience and learn the lessons involved. Learn to honor your cells for the loving service they offer you.

"Photo genetic changes occur within you when you heal present or past painful experiences. You will often feel fear when your body is reminding you of old pain. The cells that hold your memories begin showing you the pain or fear that is present. Fear, being held in the sub-atomic particles within the cell comes to the light to be embraced by it. These sub-atomic particles, the building blocks of the atoms of your cells, are the very atoms you command. Does it surprise you to learn that you are in command of the very structure of the physical universe? Why should it? You all know you are one with God in your own right. Doesn't this entitle you to now own the knowledge that you are able to command the physical structure in which you house your divine consciousness?

"When you heal, fear is changed into light, new direction is given to the body and health is restored. Since you are the leader of your body, you can command your cells to do as you please, thus giving direction to the body. This is why there are those among you who can release disease from your organisms and live in apparent good health. It is good health, indeed, when your communication with the cells of your physical structure is so clear that they are happy and in-tune with your wishes and with the plan for your healthy life and ascension. Remember ascension is not the leaving of the body but traveling *with* it to other realms. Your body is made up of light, so why would you want to leave it behind anyway? I tell you truly, you could not find a better vehicle for your consciousness if you looked within a thousand universes.

"Please be aware of the difference between *command* and *demand*. You are in command of your body and of all your cells, but it will do you no good to *demand* that they do what you wish. Think of your cells as individuals, friends. Which of your friends would respond favorably if you walked up to them and demanded that they do as you wish? Within all structures, even your cells, there is a desire for oneness and cooperation. Pay close attention to the urge you have as an individual to be honored, respected and loved, and you will see what each cell desires and deserves, too.

"When you heal an atom of your body by re-programming it into the light that its highest destiny holds, you offer it the chance to experience joy anew. How do you re-program a cell? *By experiencing its inner environment with it.* To do this is a simple thing; feel what that cell is experiencing. When you unite with each cell in this way, the cell or cells in question no longer experience aloneness. When you unite your consciousness with that of each cell, or group of cells, love is present in those cells and disease cannot remain. Disease, which is fear, is changed into love. Harmony is restored and the body returns to health. It will help if you detach from the idea that you *are* the feelings the cells hold.

"I will use an example. Let us say an individual has the flu. There is much discomfort in the body. It is common for people to hate the condition their body is experiencing, thereby hating the afflicted cells. This perpetuates the condition. On the contrary, if each afflicted cell is embraced and *accepted* for what it is choosing to manifest, then peace prevails and the body is released from the grip of fear. Do you see? It is the fear that pain will continue unabated that causes so many of you to run from yourselves instead of wrapping yourselves in light. Acceptance of any condition is the precursor of healing. To hate yourself or your cells for being ill is the worst thing you can do for your body. So please, do not mistake judgement for love. Judgment of disease is abandoning the body to fear.

"Imagine that a friend is ill. Your first reaction toward them is compassion, is it not? Why then when *you* become ill is there a rush to judge yourselves? Find sympathy, compassion, and nurturing for yourselves instead. I tell you truly, when any one of you becomes ill there is always a need for more nurturing within. Use this opportunity to nurture yourself and not judge yourself. With non-judgement and love the body is always restored to harmony. How then does this apply at the cellular level?

"To experience well being and extreme health you must first be willing to feel anything that is within you at any given time with no fear of doing so. In order to heal individual cells, you must feel the emotion that each cell holds. In this way you are always willing to keep company with each cell and to give that cell love. To fear the emotions your cells contain is to hold those cells and health itself at bay. To embrace all feelings *and potential feelings* willingly is to act in accordance with the highest love for all cells. This is universal law. To do otherwise is to try to separate yourself from a part of your body. Why then does it come as such a surprise to you that the parts of yourself you have abandoned have become ill? What you fail to realize is that when you release fear from your cells (by embracing your emotions as we have much discussed in the past) you free all of your physical body to live in peace. When you do this you also experience a level of ultimate personal freedom.

"When you are ready to feel communion (oneness) with each cell (actually or potentially) you are ready for what I will call atonement. The atonement of the physical body is to reunite with the love that you are on a higher level of awareness. Please notice that, especially in this case, "atonement" is the same as "at-one-ment," or oneness. When you come across cells in your body that hold fear and are resistant to releasing it upon your command, you must step in with love and not with judgement. In this case, judgement is simply your fear that you are not more powerful than disease. You are! But only when you are in love and not in judgement of yourself or your body.

"To heal yourself of disease, mental, physical or spiritual, you must hold a high honor and regard for your own physical body. In this way, you access all your spiritual power and bring it to bear upon the affected area of your being, i. e. you are acting within the integrity of love. When you honor yourself and are able to keep company with your cells, your cells eventually return that love to you. When this occurs, all fear is released from those cells. Eventually your entire cellular structure is without fear. This, my friends, occurs in the latter stages of ascension. To experience this is to feel bliss in the entire organism. It is like each cell is having an orgasm all at once! This bliss of this goes so far beyond the sexual experience to which I analogize as to become unrecognizable. It is like living in the utter joy of being. To this, nothing in your third dimension can compare. We know you all want this. To have this you *must* embrace the physical form for the beauty of divine expression that it is.

"Accepting the beauty of your form's divine expression goes beyond mere physical attractiveness. It is nothing of this sort of thing. Beauty is not seen with the physical eye but with the whole being of light—with all "eyes" open, all parts of your consciousness. It is to see yourself and others as perfect in each exact moment of time. There is no other way to bliss. Abandoning the physical form or hating yourself for the parts you do not like will not get you there. There is no "perfect" form, in the physical, no "perfect" body. All of you are unique in your beauty of expression. Feel the truth of this, feel how palpable it is. Enjoy your unique form of light.

"Now, allow me to speak of letting go of those parts of the body that are resistant to healing by way of cooperation. Many of you are afflicted with or know beings who are afflicted with what you call cancer. Cancer is a concentrated mass of fear within the body. It is a group of cells that have decided, for a variety of different reasons, to go against the body's desire to live. It is the manifestation of utter confusion at the cellular level. Ask your microscopic doctors about this. They will confirm it for you.

"When cancer is present within you there is a need, sometimes immediate, to make a decision about choosing to live! Sometimes this means commanding the cancer to leave at once. This can take the form of removing the affected body part by medical science. This is not an unwise choice in many, many cases. It allows you as an entity to continue to live and experience future joy. Cancer and other forms of fear can be communicated with but when communication is rejected by a part of the body that has gone too long without love and acceptance then you as master of your body must choose to live. I say this to show you that your consciousness may not be ready yet to "know" that it is master of your body now and be able to heal it in a timely manner.

"When a disease is present that does not threaten your life or place you in immanent danger, much can be done to work with the afflicted cells and begin encouraging them to come back to a place of cooperation and harmony. Now, I will not say cancer and other forms of life-threatening disease cannot be healed in this way, but I do caution you not to mistake your desire to heal or your "intent" with actual healing of the body. The intent of the intellect does not heal the body. Your own divine love within you does the healing. Many of you are not yet at this stage of your development. I do not say this to discourage you but to help you be decisive in your discernment.

"Let us again speak of judgement and the need to abstain from it as a way of creating health. When you are feeling ill, you meditate: "What have I *caught* that has made me ill in such a way?" This thinking represents deep attachment to the third dimension *as source*. For those of you a bit more enlightened you think: "What have I *done* that has made me slip into old patterns of fear that my body now holds?" This is *judgement*. For those of you a bit more enlightened still: "What have I *encountered within myself* that has allowed me to revisit an old pattern of fear for the purpose of embracing it now in love? This is true wisdom because it is based in *self-love*. Love is the path to health. Judgement will avail you nothing.

"Largely, when you are ill you are in the illusion that you are less powerful than the world around you. You falsely believe your body cannot hold its own power and energy in the face of the energies more powerful than you alone. What you can now choose to understand is that you are the most powerful being in your world. It is only when you run from yourself and your own power that you fall ill. To do this is to give away your power. Many of you still give away your power to others, to third dimension, or to ideas that you are not worthy of receiving love at all times. Change this and you change not only yourself and your state of health but also the world. Believe it, for it is indeed true.

"In this moment, you are actually re-creating a dimension of much higher authority than the rigid third dimension right here, and you are doing it in your own body! Does this not excite you to your very toes? It should, it shows you what you are capable of. Even now many of you are experiencing this on a daily basis. Moments of bliss, perhaps in meditation or your journeywork as in times of old. Perhaps in the dream state, or in your heart's giving of love to another. It is a welcome state is it not? Why not embrace this as a way of living and simply enjoy it at all times?

"'How?' you say. How, indeed! There is no 'how.' It is not something you do, it is who you are that is this joy! When you know in every fiber of your being that you *are* joy, you will release all that is in your body that is not joy. You only hold fear within you because you have been told to do so by others in your realm. When you experience guilt, shame or fear of the loss of acceptance of others, this is all fear. Isn't it wise to detach from those still stuck in their old ways and fears? It is limitation. For some of you, simply knowing that you *can* do this that will empower you to do so. Remember there is no "how." There is only being and the willingness to move ahead independent of what others think of you. Do not let their low opinion of themselves hold you back.

"Let us return to your wellness and your state of being that tests you. When you are in ill health or distress of mind, it is your cells that hold this illusion. When you heal your cells, you heal yourself, body and mind. In truth, these are one anyway, but that is food for an altogether different discussion! You see, when you take responsibility for all that is within you, you begin to glimpse the real truth. Remember the three ways of looking at ill health as above. Truth is relative you see, and *none* of the above statements are actually untrue; it is just that each holds a higher light quotient than the preceding one. There are higher light quotients still, but for today we will stay with these three.

"Your body is your divine link with the Unlimited All. When you heal the body and mind, you heal *all* of you. You see, all of you are one. When you understand this, when you *know* this, you will rise to the occasion and become one with yourself. Having done this, you then take authority not only over all that is within you but over all that you see around you, commanding and giving direction in love, knowing it is you too. Remember all is one, you are one with all. All is you. Do not separate yourself to believe that the third dimension is the source of what you need or desire. You are above the third dimension and you command the physical universe. Use this knowledge to embark upon the journey of healing your physical body, turning all fear into light. Embrace your cells in the great journey of self-discovery and ultimately of self-love. It is love that changes the world and it begins within you!

"My blessings to you all as you journey to the heart of your cells and begin the process of mastery over all that you are! Peace be with you in this wondrous journey. The road awaits you."

Chapter 12

The Unifying Power of Self-Love, Cellular Healing, Part II

The second part of Kuthumi's teaching on cellular healing as it appeared in Sedona Journal of Emergence.

Let us continue our discussion on self-love. If you will remember, in Part I, we spoke of the need to love every cell and also to love the emotions contained within them in order to create healing of the body. Love is the path to health and the path to spiritual clarity. Love creates healing not only on the physical, cellular level as it changes the body into light but also in your level of conscious awareness as a spiritual being. Therefore, it is not only an important aspect of maintaining physical health but a large factor in creating a dynamic flow of energy that can take you further into multidimensional healing. It is the place where physical and spiritual healing come together thus bringing you to the gateway of multidimensional healing and cross-dimensional experience.

Many of you understand the concept of existing in multiple dimensions at once, indeed, you are multidimensional beings, are you not? You do not exist just in this third-dimensional but in many different dimensions at this moment. Because of this there must be a way to link these dimensions together. The binding fabric that allows you to experience your multidimensionality is, of course, love. If you consider how your love of each cell can heal and therefore unify the body, perhaps you can begin to see how this principle of self-love applied at all levels of being can heal the illusion of separation. Let us look at this further.

First, be willing to receive more love throughout your body and mind. Love yourself and your cells *as they are,* not how you would like them to be and this will allow you to start conceptualizing the process of consciousness unity with all dimensions. So you see, healing the body, mind, and emotions is of paramount importance if you are to experience the full extent of who you are on all levels. When you experience love on the cellular level and come to see how it heals the body, you are then ready to expand upon this to allow yourself access to the other realms. Consider the ramifications.

Multidimensional healing is actually where you begin to heal the rupture of self between levels of awareness so that you can experience the wholeness of who you are in all dimensions. This is the manifestation of oneness on the third-dimensional level. The other aspects of who you are on a soul level already know of the part of you that exists in 3D. But the 3D part of you does not experience the joining of who you are with the other dimensions. This is the manifestation of separation.

The multidimensional healing that occurs when you love yourself is the lifting of the illusion of separation as well as the *corresponding block of perception in the intellect.* You then see that you are love. You then see that everyone is love. You then see that all here in 3D is love. You as individuals are doing this in your own bodies and as a species, are doing it in the cross-dimensional realms.

When you create healing on the body level *to the extent that your cells begin to individually hold light,* there will be no gap between who you are on a physical, third-dimensional level, who you are on all levels, and who you are as God. So you see, cellular healing can bring you to a point of experiencing oneness or the lightness of being. This is what it means to be light. When carried to its furthest extent, you can begin to heal the rupture of self between dimensions called "the veil." When many of you do this you, begin lifting the structure of the planet to the next dimension or level of awareness. You do this together after you have already healed yourself.

This is exactly why the body is so important in the ascension process. You cannot reject a part of yourself and expect to remain whole. It is only fear held in the cells and communicated to the mind that tells you the physical part of you is any different or "less than" the other levels. This fear then causes you to react and reject yourself and your very nature as third-dimensional beings. It is fear that tells you this. If you embrace the fear, you will see how perfect you truly are and how equal your body is with all other forms of light that you are. The body is the third-dimensional representation of light in physical form. It is already perfect by its very nature, pure love itself, and does not need to be changed or, of course, rejected.

Disease is the fear that you are not already perfect and lovable. When you are willing to admit you *are* lovable you can see this. When you are willing to receive unconditional love you will feel this. So stop trying to perfect yourself as a way of deserving to be loved. Receive love and see how you are already perfectly deserving. It will accelerate a shift in your consciousness and ultimately allow you to gain entrance into the other dimensions.

Do you now begin to see why self-love is so vitally important? Whether on the cellular level, in the intellect or on the emotional plane, *self-love* is the irreplaceable and inescapable pathway to union and bliss—for an individual and as a species. Relax into this and feel it flow over you. Receive it now and find peace. Ultimately, it is your pathway as a planetary body of oneness. It is the hope of the world.

Self-love activates the essence of the soul in your divine consciousness and joins it to your body. It is because your soul essence *recognizes love as itself* that allows it to do this. When you are in judgment, your soul does not recognize this as a valid way of being and in fact, sees this is a false representation of who you are. Judgment is not you! The idea of imperfection is not you! Therefore, when you are in judgment of yourself, you experience separation. Judgment is like the invalid password given to your computer that does not allow you access within, access to your true self. Only love is the correct password.

Use this thought as a guide. Ask for help from the levels beyond the veil in this way: "Help me to surrender the limitation that my thoughts now hold so I do not block the flow of love into my being. Love is greater than my thoughts. I now accept the need for love in my thoughts and in my self-talk so I can receive a greater love than I have ever before imagined or experienced." This is the willingness to receive love: the willingness for one's thoughts to be changed into love and away from fear and judgment. It is the greatest single thing you can do for yourself. It will allow you to become open in your heart and mind in order for the whole being to receive the greater quantity of love that it has so far been unable to receive. Receiving love on this level is the key to happiness, prosperity, and bliss.

Happiness and prosperity on all inner levels is the precursor to the joy of surrendering to the love that awaits you. When you receive unconditional love, your whole world lightens and fear is transcended. Relief floods your body and your cells respond by beaming light outward. At its fullest expression this light is visible to others.

There are many ways to love yourself and indeed many expressions of self-love. When you love yourself you create healing on many levels simultaneously. This must occur since you are a multidimensional creation. When self-love is initiated at the base chakras by loving the most basic you in the physical, healing spreads throughout the entire form. For self-love to have its greatest effect on the physical body it must also touch the emotions and the intellect and clear all old ideas about self there, too.

It is in the intellect that self-love is often first allowed to do its work. Now, we have spoken long and hard on the matter of the emotions being the foundation of love for oneself and for others. Of course, this still holds true and is of paramount importance, but the intellect is not devoid of love for self. In fact, it is in the intellect that many of you allow the idea of self-love to be born into your being. Here, old ideas of self-worth and fears of inadequacy still hold you back.

Remember when we spoke of the human desire for a better life being one of the highest forms of creation? Indeed it is. Is not desire for something more, something better, often born within the intellect? Ah, now here is where fear can take hold. At the very first stirrings of desire for a greater union with love, fear often stand in the way. It is as if a great barrier blocks your path to a greater knowing of self as love. Think of it this way: You desire to feel better about life and about yourself, but as soon as you desire this, a fear of not being worthy jumps up to block you. This fear will often disguise itself as the truth. It will tell you that you do not deserve to receive love from others and from God, even from yourself. It will falsely tell you to turn away from receiving.

At this point, many of you turn back. In the process of believing these lies, you hide from the very truth that will set you free. Think of this: If it is unconditional love you wish to receive then nothing, *nothing* can keep you from it except your own free will choice. When you see a puppy or a kitten, soft, furry, gentle and playful, full of love and curiosity do you not instantly love it? This is how God sees you. Your immaturity, your "imperfections" are as lovable as the antics of a puppy. You are as wondrous and as completely lovable as a newborn kitten. Indeed, you are loved such as this.

Is not unconditional love free to you by its very definition? Why then do you stutter and stammer when it is offered to you? Love sees the places where you fail, where you hold back; it sees all. It loves all of this about you. It does not ask you to change. If you stayed exactly the way you are now for all of eternity, you would still be so beautiful to love, to God. Is not God *love*? Embrace the wondrous miracle of love that is offered to you and receive. Receive love now.

Indeed, it is the God within your *own* being that desires to set you free and unite you with the God of the universe and give you all the love you so richly deserve *by your birthright!* You might well ask, "Is not the God of my being the same as the God of the universe?" Indeed it is! I separate these two, for the sake of argument, to show you an important fact: If you can allow the God of your being (yourself) to love you, then you can receive all the love that exists in the universe! Do you see? Self-love is the key!

It is not God that casts you aside for your failings but your very own intellect that does so. Unfortunately, many of you *believe it is God doing this.* When you allow the fear in your intellect to turn you away from self-love, you automatically turn away from love that is offered to you from outside your awareness. This creates situation after situation that brings you only as much love as you can give yourself—only as much love as you are willing to receive with the conditions *you have placed upon yourself.* But when you increase the love you feel for yourself, the world *must* reflect this by sending more love your way from the "outside."

How do you change your perception and begin receiving? It is done so by using the most powerful tool you possess: your freewill. When you accept the desire that you wish to experience more love, you can then say to God, "I wish to receive more love." This is what many of you have already done. Indeed, we in the realms of love do often hear this request shouted to us each day, dare I say, every moment? We do hear you and give you all the love you desire. The problem occurs when you become unwilling to receive it! Asking for love and being willing to receive it are two entirely different things.

Here is where we come back to the concept of self-love and how it plays out in your daily life. When the intellect acknowledges the need for more love and you ask, "May I have more love, please?" Though this is not how many of you phrase it! It is you who block the love we send in response. The intellect, in responding to the fears or supposed imperfections you see within you, causes you to instantly turn away from the idea of actually having what you ask for. It is you who create the roadblocks.

It saddens us to see you do this since we must honor your freewill. Do you see? It is you who block the gift with a myriad of excuses for doing so. Most of these excuses sound something like this: "I am not loving enough to deserve more love," or "I am too fat," or "I am bad," or "I am not smart enough," or "I am not worthy of being in the presence of God." The reasons are as infinite as your imagination. Isn't it God's choice to give you love or not? Who are you to decide you are not worthy to receive love when God desires to give it? Do you contain this wisdom in your intellects? No, you do not. Now, do not use *this* as another excuse not to receive love either!

If you live in your fears there will always be a reason to not receive love. If you live in your desire to receive, your free will, you will always allow yourself to receive love beyond even your own *ability* to do so. Receiving love from the divine is not within your own capability. Did you know this? Indeed, are you not so full of fears that it will always turn you away from receiving? It is so with all, my friends. All of you have reasons that are not so different from each other that would keep you from believing it is all right to receive unlimited love. How to receive love is not as important as your desire to do so.

When you think about wanting more love and are unable to experience it after repeated attempts simply do this: Ask yourself if you are *willing* to receive. If you are willing to receive love then it must be so, since you now are not trying to do it on your own but do so with God's help. Becoming willing to receive is to ask for help in doing so. If you are willing to receive, you are open to receiving help.

Coming to understand these things allows you to see beyond the old dogma that says you are separate from love or from each other. It cannot be any other way. When you change your thoughts, you change your perception. You are connected with your thoughts and your feelings are you not? It is why it is so terribly important that you face your thoughts and fears and embrace your feelings instead of run away from them. Those whom you call mentally ill are far more aware than many of you realize but they separate themselves from their thoughts, their own thoughts they cannot live with or love. The thoughts and feelings most of you separate yourselves from create the illusion of separation. It is a mistaken belief that your feelings are more powerful than you are. If you embrace them, you will not be overwhelmed and controlled by your emotions. You own them. It is not the other way around. You are the master. So your feelings will at times be painful and disturbing or unruly and flamboyant. So be it! You embody in all ways the miracle of unlimited creation. Accept this and be who you are.

When you embrace your thoughts and emotions, you create intimacy with self on a profoundly deep level, causing the very cells of your body to change their genetic structure into light. It cannot be any other way. You see, the cellular structure is such that as you grow in wisdom, as you grow in the understanding of your true nature you *must* become light. By being loving with yourself you exist in joy and allow yourself to be in bliss—the emotion's reaction to the knowledge of self as love. By doing this, you re-configure your cells, teaching them to mirror who you are in spirit: light.

When you are in love with yourself, you are in harmony with your thoughts and feelings and in-tune with the divine. As you would say, you are in-touch with yourself. This is you before the fall from grace, you in oneness with yourself. It is only when you separate yourself *from* yourself—from your thoughts and feelings—that you experience difficulty. When you are separate from your own thoughts and feelings, you lose your joy. You are in separation. Since divine thought created the universe, being in harmony with your own thoughts and feelings, ultimately, in harmony with your divine thoughts you will re-create the universe once more. The divine timing of this will unfold shortly. It is not that your world will change so much, it is just you will feel differently about absolutely everything around you because you will see that everything *is* you.

Think of it this way: God—or that which you call God and currently separate yourself from—created the world and you in it. Now think of your bodies as the world and yourself as God. You created your bodies so that you would have a place to intimately experience this physical realm that you are now having a relationship with. When you can take credit for creating your bodies and love them, you can begin your ascension. Now, remember all my teachings that have come before. You do not do this with your intellects, far from it. You do this with your wholeness in thought, spirit, body and heart. Hear me, do not misconstrue this understanding or many of you will be once again lost in the illusion of your minds. Third-dimensional mind is but a reference point for you to hold your divine matter together once you created it in the first place. Third-dimensional mind is just the casing on the sausage. It is *you* who is divine, so worship your intellect no more! Worship your true self in body, heart *and* intellect, seeing and valuing all for the different parts they play in this drama.

If you will embrace yourself in love, become willing to receive more love, we offer you a constant and ever-growing experience of being loved. When you are so full of love that you think you can contain no more, you will let go and see that you are love itself. This is a most joyous experience on all levels, in all forms of emotion, body, intellect and spirit. It is indeed the oneness we speak of.

We have spent quite enough of your time for now but will continue to teach and share with you the ways of love available to you if you will only but open up to receive. Cast aside all reason to be loved. Let go of why it would be all right to be loved and receive. Surrender the old barriers and roadblocks that convince you that you are not lovable, and receive. Become willing to receive and it will truly be so. Allow what you wish for most to become not only possible but ultimately yours.

Begin living forever in love, experiencing unending increase of love and living in the proof of your own mastery: being love itself. To do this you must allow yourself to receive from us and from all those around you. Begin now. Receive now. With gentle hearts and a profound love for you we give you this now. Let the receiving of love be the proof to you of your worthiness. Be in peace, my friends, and so it is.

Chapter 13

Living in the Magic, Cellular Healing, Part III

Kuthumi's teaching on cellular healing as it appeared in Sedona Journal of Emergence.

Greetings, fellow masters of the light. We welcome you to the Oneness of All. Today we will talk about living in the realm of miracles, which is to say, being the magic of who you are. Are you ready to transcend the veil and ascend to your next level of being? Indeed many of you think you are.

Have you integrated the teachings that have come before this one about loving your cells and then loving all of your imperfections? In truth you really have no imperfections, you just think you do. Have you opened up the lines of communication with your cells? Have you prepared your pathway of self-acceptance? These things are essential if you are to become whole in your awareness of self as divine.

You are eternal beings of great light and because of this it is important you understand that living with miracles as everyday occurrences is what you came here to do. How do you go about learning to be open to miracles? You must become very good at receiving. This means if you have any issues about not receiving because you don't believe you deserve it, these false beliefs must go. Receiving is not about performing or measuring up to some illusory standard. It is about receiving the gift of grace. Grace comes to you as a gift from God to remind you of who you are.

When you are willing to be open and receive these great gifts from God, the next choice you face is becoming willing to believe God loves you so much that God is willing to give you a miracle every day. Every single day! In fact, each day already contains many, many miracles, but you are not used to understanding this so you dwell on what is negative instead of looking up to receive. The belief in the miraculous is the only choice, the only pathway to bliss, the only pathway to ascension to the fifth dimension. The emotions, in their subtle, intimate and persistently loving way, lead you to this great leap—the leap into magic. This is the leap into miracles and into grace.

Do you have a desire to live in the place where miracles are the order of the day? Many of you carry a profound sadness because you believe in this but cannot experience it and experience separation instead. I have such compassion for your suffering and struggling and still much love to give you. I know what it is like to live in the third dimension. Please know you are close to the end of your pain, but when you separate yourselves from the faith that is your pathway to unlimited joy, you fall prey to fear. Even your bodies communicate this to you through many different illnesses and discomforts.

Living in the realm of the miraculous allows you to not only believe in magic but to live miracles every day. To believe all things are possible and to experience this directly with your whole heart, mind and body is to be open to receiving. Indeed, this is the truth of who you are! You are beginning to wake up to this great truth. When you finally and forever refuse to "settle for less," miracles will manifest for all of you.

We in the higher dimensions of love already experience your world as bountiful and perfect. Buddha sees the third dimension as all beauty, all joy and full of laughter. All is love and nothing needs to be changed—least of all you. It is living in this awareness that you all desire. This is the same energy as walking on fire. Many of you have taken fire walks have you not? To do this is to live in the manifestation of the miraculous, of mind over matter, of spirit over the physical. This is the joy all of you seek but it cannot be won, conquered, or earned.

Every day is a gift and to know this in your heart of hearts is to live in the magic of each moment. Wake up in the morning and say to yourself, "I am ready to walk into my miracle for today. I am willing to have my eyes opened to see what the miracle is and I let go of all expectations." Be ready for your miracle today and be ready for another one tomorrow.

Miracles come in all forms. Don't try to anticipate what the miracle will be. Life itself is a miracle, my friends! Don't demand or dictate what your miracle will be or what it will look like. I do *not* advise you to say "I will receive my miracle of divine partnership in human form: my soul mate will now knock on my door!" Or, "I will win the lottery!" This is ludicrous, of course, but unfortunately it is how many of you still live. Trying to force your intellects to direct the flow of divine thought and magic is useless. The energetic frequency of your intellect is far to low to manifest objects into third dimension. However, your heart held open in a place of receiving can easily be led to the gifts of the day. To become a better receiver, ask for your blocks to be shown to you so that you can let them go.

Remember the power of the human desire? When you desire things, even material possessions on a mundane level, you take a step forward toward your leap into other realms and create a new pathway for yourself. When you feel the need to move on to more fulfillment you can even create new choices that you could never before have imagined. When your desire for more is felt and expressed there is always response from God. When the desire for unlimited living is expressed, the response from God is to give you a miracle! It's that simple. But you must do this in humility and without ego, not for selfish gain but for the purpose of living more in harmony with yourself and with others.

"Can God do this for me?" many of you ask. Of course! It is easy for God to do this. What you should be asking yourself is, "Can I receive it?" Am I willing to become vulnerable in order to receive? Usually, the answer is no. Does this surprise you? It shouldn't, most of you have a tough time responding to the gift of love being given to you even in small quantities such as is customary in the third dimension. Most beings of your realm do not usually give out unconditional love to others, especially those they do not know personally. In our realm, it is common to love *all others* as you would love yourself or as you would desire to be loved.

For those not yet experiencing daily miracles, take heed, the realm of the miraculous is close at hand. It is as close as your own desire to live more freely and more fully in joy. Many of you now feel that if your life doesn't change soon, it is not worth living. Your earthly, third-dimensional life is no longer palatable or even remotely satisfying to you. These feelings are not the same as the hopelessness of the past; they are the inevitable acceptance of the desire to live beyond the daily toil of 3D. Soon you will notice that every cell of your being desires this change to the miraculous. Let me explain.

You are approaching a bridge it has come time to cross. You must face your enemy. It is as if you are facing your twin and he or she is saying, "I don't believe in miracles!" with feet firmly planted on the ground and refusing to budge. There exists the potential within all of you to be negative, cynical, sarcastic, and resistant. These are the opposite of faith. It is faith that allows you to take action when you are scared, tired and hopeless. Begin not only believing in faith but also in miracles and live in magic. Begin living this way now and receive all that you require.

Faith is what allows you to do things like walk on fire. But faith as a belief system or thought is not enough. *You must learn to take action on your faith!* When you take a step into fire and walk out onto the hot coals, you are in a state of grace. You are *living* your faith. This is what it means to receive grace, to take the action steps your faith allows you to take. This is the leap, and it must be taken anew each and every day as you face your negative thoughts, fears, and illusions about life. Trust they are only false beliefs or fears; trust that you are loved, provided for, guided and protected. This is what allows you to transcend the veil and *live* in the state of grace. Each moment you trust and take action believing you are loved and provided for, you become ready to experience the miracle.

Living your faith means to live the resiliency that never gives up. This is what will shift many of your illnesses and imbalances. To live your faith is to embrace life fully and engage all of your desires, goals and dreams. It is to look at your physical existence as a gift, a very fragile gift, and be able to walk the thin line between life and death—to live each moment with complete joy even if there is no next moment. This is to walk the razor's edge. If you fear death, you cannot do this. If you fear failure, you cannot do this. If you fear pain, you will not do this.

When you choose to live in lack, evading your dreams, you avoid the very emotions that lead you to peace and create separation with yourself. If you embrace your fears, love them and celebrate who you are even in the face of fear, you are ready to begin. To live fully and in faith is to embrace all emotions and not turn away from yourself in defeat. The sadness that is endemic to the human experience is the experience of separation. When you are ready to face this within yourself and face the fear of failure, you are ready to receive help. Realize, my children, that sadness is not to be avoided but cherished and loved as a part of your humanness. Then experience the joy that is there to behold, the joy of self-acceptance.

The goal is to feel the sadness of separation while simultaneously accepting that it is small compared to what else you have in this life. To do this is to leap across the veil. To push away the sadness instead of embracing it and choosing not to let it get you down is to run away from yourself. To embrace the sadness as a way of accepting life is to begin the process of believing in miracles. Accept your fragile humanity as it is and realize that you are powerless to change it. Then take a leap in your faith and receive a miracle!

This is difficult for many of you. Many of you would rather escape from the entire experience of being human instead of finding acceptance of it. If you run away from being human where will you go? You have an Earth expression, "Wherever you go, there you are." Running away from yourself does not get you into "heaven." It is does not allow you to cross the veil into joy. In fact, it is the joy you run away from.

To believe in magic is to embrace the totality of sadness, grief and loss in your life and still believe that the power of love is greater. This is the miracle of life. It is what you are looking for. It is the proof of your faith. When your faith is as great as this, you will leap across the chasm of fear and discouragement and live in the realms of reawakened joy. And it all begins with accepting yourself. Most of you are too hard on yourselves. Remember to play more because play is the pathway toward self-acceptance.

Once you begin experiencing the magic of life and start *recognizing* the miracles that are occurring in your life every day, you are ready to begin encountering your true essence as spirit. As this happens, you will feel an acceleration of your body's wellness and the remaining fear your cells are holding will be thrown off. Do not become worried when you feel sadness or grief in this process. It is just your remaining fears leaving your cells. Remember, as with all letting-go, when fear leaves your body, grief is felt and you rise in vibration and in joy. This is the beginning of your ascension.

Ascension is the process of detaching from the low vibration of the third dimension and consistently choosing the vibration of love in the fifth dimension. This choice to detach is not limited to your life of the past but will always continue to include anything in your life now that is of low vibration. It will include leaving relationships that do not honor you as spirit. It will include letting go of old patterns of fear that your body still holds and surrendering the entire array of old visions you held before that said life is not joyful. In consistently choosing to honor your desire for a loving life that holds joy for you, you must let go of anything that drains your energy, dishonors you, sells you short, limits you, or abuses you. These actions are not of the fifth dimension and do not come from love. Only you can make these choices for yourself.

In your ascension process, as your cells hold more light, it is as if your essence comes nearer to your physical form. In truth, it is who you are and is always "attached" to your body. You do not feel it because your vibration is too low and you hold much fear, which obstructs your vision and sensitivity. When you rise in love, detaching from what does not honor you in the third dimension, you begin surrendering to the truth of who you are, which is spirit. When this happens, you begin transcending your personality.

What does it mean to transcend your personality? It is to experience firsthand the oneness of existence while still in a body here in 3D. At first, the experience is fleeting, a sensation of floating above while still anchored here. It is most pleasing. For others, it is to engage all that you encounter here with love as a basis of interaction. You feel what others feel, but it does not distract you from your own sense of peace. For still others, it is a feeling of self-acceptance and peacefulness that allows you to know you are loved.

The transcending of your personality does not come all at once. At first, it is an experience that prepares you to let go of more of what attaches you to 3D. As you begin to become familiar with yourself as spirit and not as your ego or personality, it becomes second nature to you. It is then is easier to trust that love awaits you in the fifth dimension. The more you are able to embrace your fear and allow your cells to fill up with light, the more your essence will become clear to you. It will almost seem as if it floats over to you to embrace you in love.

If you allow yourself to be afraid of feeling fear, you become filled with it and it blocks the experience of oneness with your essence. It will appear to you as if your very essence moves away from you. If you embrace your fears, however, release yourself from their grip, and move toward self-acceptance, your whole body is bathed in self-love. This is when you sense your essence very close. In truth your essence *is* love. It is the part of you that is consciously connected to God. It is the expression of your free will choice to love God, be loved by God, and be as one. You cannot perceive your essence when you are in fear. Your essence is the very opposite of fear, and thus they cannot coexist. This is the experience of separation.

When you allow your physical body, your mind, and your heart to be bathed in love, you will always feel connected to your essence and live in the higher realm. You will intuitively know what is going to happen in your life, you will walk toward it with faith, and you will awaken each day to greet another miracle. You will feel love all the time, you will live in the presence of the divine, and you will know that you are love.

You must completely let go of the concept of deserving to experience this. You must say: "It does not matter to me anymore if I deserve it, I will simply receive it because I desire to be loved." *The simplicity of this is the same as always: letting go and allowing.* Then love flows to you from God and crosses paths with the sadness that remains in your heart concerned with deserving, being alone, and being abandoned. As the love comes in, the sadness will leave; you will feel it, let it go and receive love in its place. Allow your body to be filled with this love from God.

If there are any ailments in your body that still do not heal, begin now to allow more love to flood in and show you what you still fear letting go of. Your cells are ready to do this. Just let it go. This is what will begin changing the fabric of your life. You will start allowing yourself to receive joy without regard to whether or not you deserve it. Most of you still check in with your personalities to see if more love is deserved before receiving. Stop this! Just receive regardless of deserving.

Remember this also. Do not try to return the love you receive by "being of service to God." This is a thinly veiled disguise of fear. It is you who fear receiving so you try to earn God's love by working for it in service. Stop this too. If you desire to do things to "help" others, and it brings you joy, then so be it. Though in truth all others on Earth are already perfect and do not need your "help." But do this *after* you have received enough love for yourself. Receiving is the *first* thing you should do, not the last.

Many of you are ready for this propitious step that can only be called a leap into faith. Simply by being present in the world as spirit, the third dimension as you know it will begin to change so rapidly that miracles will wash over everyone. Many who never knew a moment of faith will be changed—not because you will change them but because they will see the *living proof of your faith* with such clarity that they will be swept up into the movement of love that begins to conquer fear in the Earth.

Many of you ask, "How do I have more faith?" It is a good question! You alone do not create faith. It is a gift. Didn't you know this? It is a gift from God. You *cannot* create more faith; you can only ask for it and receive. Most of you would benefit greatly if you started asking for this.

When you receive faith, you begin loving yourself more. When you love yourself, it then becomes much easier to love others. You will begin doing this as a natural flow of events. Begin now by becoming taken up into the flow of love and carried along into the waiting arms of your own faith. Living in your faith will make you strong. It will bring you peace. Watch and see how many other people are drawn to you when you begin doing this. You will soon become a vehicle for others to receive more faith and they will follow in your footsteps. The proof of your faith will be all around you— miracles waiting to happen. Allow the constant flow of the love of God to sustain you. Believe in this and you will receive miracles into your life.

It is easy to believe in God. But do you believe that God believes in you? This is the decision to which you must come. You must realize with all of your being that God believes in you so much that you will be loved, cherished and honored no matter what your current state of affairs, no matter what you look like, no matter what you act like, it is unconditional and unlimited. Ask for it and receive it now. Make a decision to begin believing that miracles happen every day…to you! Do this and you *will* receive; do this and you will begin living the miracle of each moment, one moment at a time. Then grace will be yours.

May each of you live in the peace that surpasses understanding, have joy untold, and live in the certainty that you are loved, for indeed you are! Be well, my beautiful ones. Thrive in the love that abounds around you, and we shall meet you on the road to joy.

CHAPTER 14

SURRENDER TO LOVE

Channeling Kuthumi is such a joy I could not resist the urge to include another of teachings. Though this piece is from 1999, our connection had already become quite strong. When I channel Kuthumi, it is as if I can almost see him standing up in front of a great crowd imparting knowledge and leading others to the light. I always see him as a great learned person. Though this describes him only in part, it is a good image of him to offer.

Relax, receive, and let him into your hearts. He has a way of making you think that spiritual learning is a piece of cake. It's as if he can climb right into your brain, rearrange a few gray-matter cells and make it all perfectly clear to you what the nature of the universe is all about. "Have fun and enjoy the learning," he would say.

* * *

Kuthumi, channeled in June 1999, as appeared in Sedona Journal of Emergence.

Many of you have already sampled communion, union with your spirit guides and those masters in the higher dimensions. They have been your touchstones with bliss. It is now time to begin understanding exactly who they are in relation to you. Did you know you are their equals in every sense of the word? Indeed, *they* consider you so. It is time you consider yourselves so as well.

In the now moment of eternal union with All That Is, all of you are one. That is what you call God. God is not a single being, but a joining of all that is love. You love do you not? Indeed, do you not love those masters and teachers in the etheric who guide you so devotedly? Why would you presume to separate yourselves from them? They would never do so with you. It is a process to understand this, a process in which you have been absorbed for centuries. It is now time to take a giant leap ahead in your understanding of this.

You have become more comfortable in your relationships with the masters in the etheric. You now see that in the concept of "no separation," beyond the illusion of duality, an aspect of you occupies the identical space they occupy. Now you must come to understand that you are one with them. It is not a brain understanding, however; it is a *feeling* understanding. Much as you would discover a new hand on your body that you did not see before, you now discover there are many aspects of your spiritual body in which you are not as well versed, as you would think.

To continue in the illusion that we are separate is to stay in the judgment of the third dimension. You are judging yourself as "less than" or less equal to me. This is untrue. Let us be one in thoughts and hearts. In this, we shall be one in love. Is being one with love not a desired goal for all of you? At least you all proclaim this to be so. Embrace your equality then, and embrace love as it is within you, as it is within me. Let it begin by closing the ranks that exist between us (in your mind) and we will come to a central point where we *both* exist so that neither I come to you nor you to me, but we meet on equal ground and join our very natures.

You have tasted enough limited interactions that it is now time for you to begin sampling the oneness that many doors open upon. You could spend more time meeting ascended beings on the other levels. This invitation is now extended to you. In some ways, it challenges the very boundaries of what is finite. It could be said you are "pushing the envelope" or going beyond the limit of what has been done before.

All of you must know by now that when your year 2000 arrives, it will come with many vibrational openings not now available to you. It is time to prepare for what is inevitable—your inescapable joining with each other in third dimension and with us in the other dimensions. This is the plan. The plan is for oneness; the plan is for love—unilateral love, on all levels. Will you be ready to participate? You must now prepare by surrendering your old thoughts of low self-worth, separation, and fears of abandonment and confusion. All are thinly veiled forms of fear.

So come, be within *my* body as you have invited me to be in yours. Will you come with me to be in my etheric space? Indeed, you must leave your own identity in order to do so.

You might well ask, "What does it mean to leave my old identity?" It means to give up the role as "Jane," Stephen," or "Sandy." In times past, you've identified yourselves as your personality. But I say to you, your concept of who you are is most limited. It must now change. It is not enough to be "Stephen, the wise teacher." Or, "Jane, the spiritual being." You must be Spirit. *It is who you are.* The personality was just a way of describing the body and intellect, even at times, the emotions. Emotions are the most important aspect of your humanity, but the most important part of *you* is spirit. It is what you truly are. Do not be mistaken though, being spirit does not mean you cease being physical. It means you allow the two to become one.

You have all been relying too heavily on your personalities in order to have relationships with each other. In this there has been much conflict as well as confusion on both personal and planetary scales. *You are not your personality.* You are Spirit; you are God. You are Love. It is time you began acting as such. Love can permeate time, space or any aura or object. Love is all. Let yourselves be all and experience the joy of it, the bliss of oneness it is.

No longer will you use your ego or personality to define who you are. It is not unlike when an actor steps off stage. She becomes who she is beyond the role she has always played. She assumes her true identity. It is time you all do this now. You will then be more prepared for what is to follow in the next millennium.

To give up your personality does not mean allowing who you are to be lost in a vast affliction of confusion with other souls or spirits all giving up who they are. No! It is to *heighten* your sense of self as divine, securing forever your identity as the spirit you are, *and then* find communion in love.

When you love another person in third dimension, you do not give up your identity, do you? I think many of you have been working very hard to hold on to your identities in the face of much human co-dependence. You have done well. But it is now time to take your new-found freedom, your new-found identity and go exploring in the realm of spirit to see who you can find there to form new relationships with in love, beyond identity of personality, beyond the limitation of ego.

Ego insists you must be who you were in the past—a foolish and false consistency. Love encourages you to be all that you are in the now moment, beyond past and future, beyond time—it is not linear. Personality will hold you to a fixed identity of views, opinions and ideas. Spirit will allow you to be an ever-increasing new flow of creation in joy, a wellspring of growth and happiness, ever embracing more of your own being.

Even though I hold for you an identity of Kuthumi, beyond this I am love itself. And so are you. This is how we can merge in bliss. If I were to hold on to my identity of Kuthumi, I would not be able to surrender to the trust that is love and merge with you. Many of you have felt my presence with you; you have felt the love I engage in with you, but you often mistakenly credit *me* with all the accomplishment in the encounter. Don't you see, it is a mutual union? If you had not already been willing to entertain, at least in part, your equality with me, we would not experience each other's presence at all.

Interaction in the etheric realms is always a *coming together,* not simply my coming to you. Certainly in the beginning of our relationship, I could offer you a greater part of me than you could offer of yourself. But as you learned of love, trusted, and came to know this as who you are, you were able to merge with me as I could with you. You could then come to meet me part way.

What I suggest to you all now is to meet me *half way*. Many, so many of you would now be capable of this if you will only believe in yourselves a tiny bit more. You are so close and so little stands in your way of our truly joining with each other. Let our souls unite, and allow the sparks to be seen and felt around the world as we touch. We—you and I—will be an inspiration to those who yet feel separated and alone. We will unite the world in love. Our joining will be an example of what is possible for others if they will only have hope and trust that they will fulfill their own dreams of love.

Call now to your side whichever guide or master you feel closest to, and tell them that you are ready to receive and to *give* love in blissful union of the truth of your beings, in blissful truth of your One Being. Share in the joining as an equal partner. It does not matter if you feel as wise or as loving as they are. You have much grace that surrounds you; surely, you must know that. Receive the joining as grace, not accomplishment. Though you do the work, it is your spirit, not your personality, which allows the joining.

I see that many of you are ready and willing, indeed, eager to do this, so let me give you a few suggestions: When you think of giving up your identity, you often lock yourself into it instead. In *thinking* about it you have already anchored yourself more firmly within its limitations. It is a tricky thing. You simply need ask yourself, "What would it be like to experience *being* Kuthumi?" Ask with your feelings not your thoughts. Be me.

Play with it. I do not mind. You do me no disrespect in the process. Believe me, I am not offended. Indeed, I am flattered!

Use your curiosity to guide you. Use your heart to balance you. Use your thoughts to stimulate you. When all is in readiness, move away from that which you were to that which you are. Be open to finding out who you are *beyond* what you already know of yourself. Take a risk; that is what is required. Jump into the unknown. It is then you will experience for yourself a part of *you* which is unknowable! The vastness of your being awaits you in the miraculous realm of magic. You are nothing less than this.

Another simple exercise could be done. Feel your love for another. It could be for a being with you there in the physical or it could be for one of your beloved guides in the etheric. Choose for yourself. Feel your great love for someone. Feel it in a quiet space within yourself. Then, move toward the love you feel, come close to it, intimately so. Then *be* the love you feel for the other. If it helps, feel or visualize yourself moving away from your body. Do you see the distinction between feeling love and being love? Have fun with it. It will delight you. The experience of being love is the most joyful thing in the universe that you can do with your being.

Practice this with your friends. Be the love you feel for each other. Do it together and experience new levels of intimacy you never thought possible.

When you have mastered being love for another, try being the love of many people. Perhaps when you are in a group, meditating or dancing, be the love that is shared between all present. It is the best antidote for being lonely. Once you experience this, you will never feel lonely again! The experience is similar to feeling what it is like to no longer be human but a point of light. You cannot anticipate it; you can only be open to it.

Many of you have approached a point where you can do this in your meditation. It is now time to entertain these things in your waking state. The goal of the end of your old millennium is to be a walking wide-awake being of love! The goal of the new millennium is to bring this to each other and share it on a global scale.

The transition from meditation to a waking-state connection with your true essence is one that is precipitated by a clear thought of holding your individuality supreme above all else. Finding your uniqueness, allowing it to be your guide and honoring who you are allows you to step into your essence in a waking state. In meditation, you are obstructed from applying all of who you are to the world. You may dream, desire, and feel much in meditation, but it is still an abstraction.

Indeed, you may well say, "It is no abstraction, for me it is truly what I feel in joy, bliss and connection." Anything that does not allow you to function as a human being in third dimension while simultaneously functioning in spirit is an abstraction according to third dimension, is it not?

Your greatest purpose here is to bring all of who you are to bear *in* third dimension. This cannot be done by leaving it. It must be done by infusing it with who you are. So do not say, as so many these days are saying, "Please take me home, I cannot tolerate the other beings here, I wish to escape to peace." Peace will not come by escape. Do not run away from your own goal. Do not seek to escape what you yourself came to accomplish.

There is no escape from the third dimension as you know it. There is only a deepening of your intimacy with it through the infusion of your own spirit. Yield to the essence of your own higher self to know peace. To find peace, give up your old ideas of who you are. You are much more than you realize, and you will understand this when you surrender.

You do not do this by way of a linear construct. It is a construct of your own dimension that you call home. Indeed, for most of you reading this, third dimension is not your native soil. Many of you came from the fifth, sixth, and seventh plane for the purpose of bringing more light and energy to the third plane. It is why so many in the Earth plane are drawn to you.

To do this is a matter of hope. With hope, you admit to being powerless and must therefore give up the definition of power in third dimension. When you do this, you realize that the work must be done beyond who you are in 3D. In order to achieve this end, you must begin experiencing who you are outside of your identity as Mary, Thomas, or Kathy, outside of your personality.

It is not the same as just experiencing yourself outside of your physical body. Even so, you are still your personality; you are just who you are in your old identity but out of your body. You must become that which up to now you did not think you were. You must feel it! Feel the change. When you do this, you see you are indeed quite fluid and not static as you once supposed. You are always a new creation. You are not just one physical being my dears, you are many, you are love.

Love is always flowing and changing. So you must be also. It is a task worthy of your attention. Allow who you are to change. Allow who you are to flow into nothingness, into the beingness of love.

If the task seems too monumental to you, think about this: *You* don't have to do it. You, Walter, Michael, Richard, don't have to do it. It is your essence that does it. Receive it by grace; open to it slowly, then quickly, then embrace the love that you are. Love is action. Love is creation. Love is change and love is risk. That is the key. Allow the love that you are to take the action for you. Receive it; experience it. Let the bliss flow from "outside" of you to inside of you, from inside of you to all of you. You are all one. Be one. Be love and know bliss. The new freedom awaits you. It is who you are.

My blessings are with you all. You are a part of me and my love is never ending and is never apart from you.

Chapter 15

Mother Mary's Blessing

With so many masters to communicate with, it is hard to say I have a favorite. Still, there is one I am closer to than the rest, and that is Mother Mary. I have come to know her in all kinds of ways. She is my counselor and the best listener I have ever known. She will sit patiently with me for hours and never saying a word, guide my heart and thoughts to a peaceful place or to a place where insight is possible after a long period of confusion and lack of insight.

Many people do not understand how it is possible for a psychic and channel with connections such as mine to experience periods of confusion or lack of connection, but I do. Though I have access to all the masters on the other side, I am still human and because of this I, too, occasionally go through my own growth issues. There have been times when in my own process of growth I have called out to Mary, and she has been there in a way like no other. As you can see in the appendix, she is capable of crossing the veil so completely that I feel her physical presence next to me. This has happened many times.

During a particularly difficult period in my life I spent many hours crying to release old fear and sadness. During this period, I would often feel Mary's presence to be with me. It was during this period that I channeled "Let Me Be Your Comforter." It was not only a piece for others, but a channeling that reassured me like no other words could. Mary backed up every word in that channeling with her presence. I know she has done this with many people since.

Once, while in a period of confusion in my life, I called out to Mary for companionship and comfort. It came to me that her love was like no other person I knew in the physical world, and I found myself wanting her company instead of a physical companion or listener. I marveled at this. I was feeling alone at the time and yet wanted no being other than her to even be with me. In that moment, I knew she was absolutely real to me. How else could I have forgone the choice of a "real" person to keep me company? I have come to understand in my work that "real" is relative. How many times have I had a physical companion disappoint me? Maybe somewhere deep in my knowing, I knew Mary could never do this.

At that time, in the moment I was choosing her over a human companion, I also accepted I might have to forgo the physical hug I desperately desired. I knew my need for a hug, however, was just me asking for proof that I was loved. I chose to accept this on faith instead. In that instant of my faith, much to my amazement and utter joy, I felt Mary's arms around me—physically! I felt a flowing warmth, physical heat, and pressure all around me. I felt her presence so much the small room, I was in filled up with a hope I can only call "sunshine." I felt as if my entire burden was lifted, and though I knew I would do my part in continuing to be being human by feeling many more things to come, still, I have never felt alone from that moment.

I asked Mary about this once, and she told me her love for us is such that she regularly crosses the veil to penetrate our hearts when we call. This was the beginning of my deep and profound trust for her in this lifetime. Since that day, I have often felt her physically with me in times of need. I have never felt so loved as I do by her.

I know may people whose lives Mary has changed. Her love is able to so completely penetrate the barriers we put up that few who connect with her are able to withstand her loving presence. There are usually no dry eyes present when I channel her in group. She is so gentle that even the toughest characters soften and the strongest walls fall.

Many people for whom I have channeled her ask me about Mary being the mother of Jesus. I explain that bringing another master into the world is only one of her attributes. To me, this does not in any way lessen her own mastery. In fact, during a group session held in December of 1999, Mary said the following about her being the mother of Jesus:

"It is time to discuss with you the details of my coming to your planet, my true nature, and how I conceived my child, the one you call Jesus.

"I came to your planet to manifest the truth of love in a completed way by containing both female and male qualities within myself. I did this in my own body when you knew me as Mary, the mother of Jesus. In the beginning, I knew oneness with God. Because I knew I was a creator equal to God, I knew I held the power of *all* creation within me. When I desired to be 'with child,' I knew I could do this in my own right, in my own power. I did not ask for it and was not told about it; I simply chose to be in oneness with All That Is me, and it was so.

"The child was not given to me. I created him with my divine knowledge of all things within me. Your church will call this heresy. I call it empowerment. You have this power within you—all of you. You are all creators equal with God. What you call the "Church" has long desired to control the power of all things in the Earth, and so it created much myth and superstition around me and my son. Much of what they have created is not the truth. But until now, you have believed it was so and have given away your power as a result.

"My original form was not physical, not even spirit as you know spirit. It was within the mind of God, that I first took form as Goddess. This is the true form that can live again upon your planet again, in and through you. God and Goddess are equal creators and as such, are equal in power with the Great One, the one you call God, Spirit, All That Is. It is right that you should know the truth now. It is time for you to take your places as creators, indeed co-creators and still the Earth of its unrest and create peace together.

"When I came to your planet, it was for the purpose of bringing forth teachings to empower all to be who they are in their own truth of love. I saw the Earth needed to have a gifted one to show everyone who they are. I was prepared to be that gifted one. But as I interacted with your cultures, I saw that the true female was not yet ready to be honored.

"So, I thought to myself, this world cannot receive me because of how they view women. So, I as a woman I birthed myself into the world as a man, which in my being, I am also. Then the world could have its teacher. I could do this because I knew that I am both male and female. And beyond that, I am neither. In this way, I could manifest as either female or male. This is the basis of the issues of empowerment for so many of you, men and women alike. It is the cause of many troubles for you. You do not know that you are all powerful in the Earth. But the Earth knows it and she honors you.

"When you honor my son Jesus, honor me as well, for we are one. When you do this, you honor yourselves as well, and you do justice to the whole of humanity—it is one, complete in itself without the need for a God that is separate. I am the Creator as are you. I was not a vessel; I am God, and so are you. Do not fear these ideas. They will bring you resolution and peace."

I always sensed something about Mary was not original to this planet and yet her form, her essence here makes me feel so satisfied about myself—a feeling that I lack nothing in my own completeness. This channeling confirmed it for me.

I am often asked to channel for people who are Jewish, and I am usually surprised when Mary "steps up" to speak. The first time this happened, I was giving a reading in my home in Montana to a woman I will call "Ruth." Ruth had just lost someone close to her and was looking for confirmation that her buddy, now on the other side, was all right. She also wanted to know the reason her friend had passed.

I relaxed myself, ready to channel, and Mary appeared to me in my mind. Her gentleness always stills any doubts I have, and I quickly stepped aside and let her speak. She did not announce herself, but reassured Ruth that all was fine with her buddy on the other side, and she was well and in joy. Tears of relief began to flow down Ruth's cheeks as she released her fear ,and I could see to how she was relaxing into the information being given. She asked Mary who was speaking.

"It is I, the one you call Mother Mary," she said. I held my breath for a moment waiting for Ruth's reaction, hoping she would not be offended. To my surprise, Ruth smiled. Light beamed out from her face as she spoke to Mary.

"I thought it was you; we've spoken before haven't we? she said.

"Yes, my child, we have." Mary beamed back at her.

Internally, I was shaking my head wondering how I could ever doubt the masters and their choices. Once again, the perfect choice had been made without my even being consulted. I was grateful for that. Thank goodness my own ego does not make the choice of who gets to speak through me!

I spoke with Ruth later, and she told me that when she first met Mary through another channel she had been a bit put off but only for the few moments before Mary began to speak. This is the phenomenon Mary brings with her, the ability to penetrate hearts and fear and leave only love in its place. Ruth knew this by having received it before. Since that day, I have no longer hesitated to channel Mary for all who will listen. I do not, in my humanness, posses her wisdom nor the ability to know who needs her. I let her decide all of that.

*   *   *

When I channel Mary, I do not always dissolve into her being like I did the day I described in the introduction. In fact, it is always a different experience, and I await each one with anticipation, wanting to know how she will surprise me next. One thing does remain constant, though. Whenever she speaks to a client of mine, before she finishes she *always* tells the client to give me her blessing. This has gone on for years. I have to say, I don't completely understand why she does this. Certainly, I already know I have her blessing for my work and my life, and I do know I have her love. And I know she knows this, too. Once quite recently, I gleaned a small part of what this is about.

As each person passes along Mary's blessing to me they bring her energy through their own body. In this way, they feel a measure of what I feel of her when I have her presence within me. This allows each person to experience a moment of transcending the physical world and being in the love of the higher realms. I also, at times, sense Mary smiling in a way I can only call sneaky, in a very cute sort of way. She is sending particles of herself all around the world this way! Imagine, the purity of Mary's love going to people all over the globe and touching still others through this.

There is one other aspect of Mary's blessing that I have noticed. When she asked people to give me her blessing, it is almost as if it elevates them in some cryptic way—perhaps unseen to them at the moment it happens. In truth, when people receive a channeling from Mary, they cannot help but be changed. I have noticed their voices soften, sense their stress leave, and their hearts open. I call it Mary's magic wand. In the world of psychic assistance and emotional help, I always tell people "there is no magic pill. You must feel your own feelings and heal like the rest of us do; after all we are still human."

So when people give Mary's blessing to me, it is as if they are performing a sacred rite. For a moment in time, they become the priest, the chalice, giving forth divine love to me. When I saw this for the first time, I knew there was more to come. Soon after, Mary began telling people to go out and bless others as if they were God. This evoked much horror in the emotions of my clients. How could they expect to be believed? Who were they to give a blessing as if they were God itself? Yet, with encouragement from Mary's loving and gentle words, they have done this and the results have been transformational.

We are all told to embrace our own divinity in these times of planetary and personal change. We know we are one with God but do not always act in that way. When we give our blessing to each other, we surrender our ego to do so. My clients tell me that it is a most humbling and at once spiritually elevating experience. The ultimate paradox: humanity and God in one. Isn't this the point?

Knowing that we do not easily accept the mantle of spiritual grace, Mary, in her wisdom, pushes us into it. She is the only master I know who could do this and get away with it. Who can resist her kind-hearted prodding? I have seen no one able to. It's as if she is asking a favor of the people she speaks with, to act in her stead. I for one have never been able to refuse her anything. I am sure she will be asking many more of my clients and audience members to do this for her.

There is so much to knowing who Mary is, I can only hope to scratch the surface here. By sharing some of my experiences with her, I hope to only whet your appetite to know more. Go to her, she is ready to receive you with gratitude and joy. She is eager to serve and please. She stands ready to cross the veil to show you her love in every tangible way possible. Let her come to you and put her arms around you. Let her love your little inner child with such a love, you will never be alone or afraid again. She is so capable of this and asks only a little in return: your companionship.

The most comforting thing I hear Mary say, and she says it often, is to join her in her heart. She says, "I have reserved a place for you in my heart.

I am longing for you to join me there so I can know the joy of your company. If you do not join me in my heart, I will miss you and a part of me will be lonely for you. If you choose not to join me here in my heart, I will feel your absence, but I will not give your space away to another. Instead, I will wait for all of eternity for you to come and be with me. That is my love for you."

I have joined Mary in this place in her heart. It is the place where I melt into her and she melts into me. It seems at the time that I am not as much in her or that she is in me but that we are truly one. This is the beginning of oneness; we are all soon to share in what is called God. Everlasting belonging and no aloneness awaits us all. I know this joining I have done with Mary is ultimately the joining we will do with each other. I can't begin to imagine the joy. If being one with her in such a tiny way as I am able brings such unspeakable bliss, who knows what more awaits us all? I look forward to that time when we will all know this.

Mary's channeling of the Goddess information and how she brought herself as Jesus into the world is the beginning of a longer piece, the rest of which I would like to offer now. If you like, reread the above section and continue below for continuity. And so we pick up where we left off:

"To believe the things I tell you will not just return your power to you but will also return your stature, your rightful place. The church would have you be mice begging for the crumbs of a holiness you already own. It would keep you enslaved to the idea of "sin," being less than God. You are not less. You are whole, and you are beautiful, and you are one being of such magnificence that your light is brighter than the brightest star in the heavens. You are ancient, and you contain the wisdom of the ages. Together you will light up universe beyond universe beyond time.

"These truths affect many areas of your lives. For those of you who have been desiring partnership and have not found it, I tell you now it is because you have desired to come into your own power first. Understand that you are more powerful than the partnership you are seeking.

Knowing this, you will never lose yourselves again. You do not fit within a partnership; the partnership fits within you. Your power is clear and beautiful and shared. This truth can be applied to all relationships.

"All these truths to open your heart. You who have been strong in your faith are now rewarded with truth. Where there is truth there is no need for faith. It was only the pathway. Now, simply and completely live in truth. It is the cornerstone of your being. It is the peace you have sought. Breathe deeply into the center of your body, and incorporate this into your awareness. Let go of the old ideas of sin and judgment and of being "less than." The church has no power that you do not give it. The government has no power that you do not give it. *No one* has any power over you that you do not give them.

"Now you see how there is no "Father" God. God is not split into male and female. It is both and neither. It was just a silly archetype given to you to take away your power. It was just one of many ideas that was placed within the consciousness of humans to disassemble the DNA. The DNA is where the truth still is. It is your power structure and holds the knowledge that you contain creation within yourselves. Allow it to come together again now in the true light of who you are. This and other old archetypes keep you all in prison. Free yourselves at last and feast on the truth! You are complete and do not need others to give you back what you already own.

"These truths allow you to move into the inter-dimensionality of your True Selves. This third-dimensional plane is *within* the other planes of existence. It is how you can exist within all of them at once. All planes are now available to you. The gateway to these planes is experience, not intellect. But knowing these great truths of who you are will now allow you to release your dependence upon your intellects and let go in order to *experience* the fullness of who you are. The truth of who you lies in experience, not in intellect. Faith is intellect. Truth is experience.

"From this point on, for all of you, it is simply a matter of allowing these new images to correct the old archetypes and rid yourselves of them and their limitation. I will compare this to your computers. If your computer has a virus—a piece of incorrect information that prevents the computer from functioning properly—you introduce new information to correct the virus. It is so with your bodies.

"The old archetype of God was introduced into your genetic programming through your intellect in the form of fear. It entered your DNA, disassembled it, and was lodged there, resulting in the surrender of your natural abilities: intuition, psychic senses, creativity, passion, and ultimately, your power. Now when the new information—the new archetype—comes, it is like an anti-virus being introduced into your bodies. It seeks out all the old archetypes and cleanses your body of them. This is done through your acceptance of the truth, the truth that you are God in oneness with each other, God in eternal play. Allow this new information to enter and interact with your ideas of who you are. Allow your DNA to return to its original design. Allow the truth to set you free.

"When your fully functioning DNA returns to you, you will find yourselves interacting with others in new ways that honor both them and you. It will allow for the predominance of win-win situations instead of win-lose conflicts. It will foster the creation of a new intimacy between individuals and a new cooperation of peoples in the world unaffected by fear of vulnerability. You will not be afraid of who you are any longer, so you will be unafraid of sharing who you are with others. There will be nothing to lose but your fear! You will be amazed at how good you feel. Fear will no longer dominate your interactions or your cultures. You are all in the process of this great awakening.

"Many of you have asked how this is to be done. There is no ceremony needed, no system of healing that will free you. It is within your own power to do this. If this were not so, it would not return you to *your own power!* Resist the temptation to give your power away *again* to another who says, "I can heal you of this." Remember: *You* can heal you of this. It is simply the higher light that you all have been working with already that does the work. The light itself will heal you. It is the light within you that does this.

"The new information, the new archetypes, are examples of the higher light that recognizes the old archetypes and kicks them out of your body. To incorporate this into your bodies, simply allow your vibration to raise. Continue whatever healing you are doing to allow your vibration to go higher and higher. There is no one specific cure, no certain procedure to do this. All manner of healing work that empowers you will work. Trust yourselves to do this. Whenever you feel your vibration lowering, move on from whatever it is that causes you to sink and find new freedom in entertaining more joy.

"Joy is natural to your being. It is part of who you are in God. If you are not experiencing joy, move along until you find it. Remember, experience is truth. Fear will often hide in the intellect and keep you from going to a higher place because of your fear of what others will think. It is your own joy that is at stake. Follow your joy. Do not give in to pressures to conform to something that does not allow you to feel joy. Become like the child who is at play and naturally expresses joy without fear.

"Many of you will wonder, after reading these words, "Why is it that Mary speaks to us so? Is she not the gentle loving Mother of all." I would say to you, Am I not the teacher of Jesus? The one who showed him his own power? The one who gave birth to the new archetype of love? But yet believe not me; believe the truth of your own bodies when you *feel the power* growing within you to be teachers also. Engage the light within you and allow it to empower you to act in your own behalves and teach the truth. Show others who you are, that you are the great light that has come to save the world from the darkness of fear.

"Where is your faith in yourselves? Believe not in me, but in you own power, and be healed. Do not look to me or to others to do this work for you; you are whole as I am. You need no other to make you so. I *am* the gentle mother, nurturer of all, yes, but I am also the Goddess, the one with all power to create. You also have this power. Allow it to be unleashed within you. It is time that you take your places. It is time that the reign of love returns to the Earth.

"I am but one of many. You are the multitudes that will create the new universe of love for all to see. You are in this great task together. Come together now in love and unite! Be called to that great purpose that you are. Be who you are now. Be love and live in peace. It is time you received what you have so long deserved: to live in peace within yourselves and with each other. Go now, create the changes that will last a lifetime, an unlimited lifetime of God and Goddess living together in love and empowerment.

Chapter 16

Finding Purity of Heart

The following is Mary's invitation to you to see yourself with the same unconditional acceptance that she does. It offers us a lifting of human propensity towards self-judgment and the result is nothing short of freedom. Breathe easier as you read her words of welcome into the spirit of the all-inclusiveness of her unconditional love. The following was channeled in October 1998, and appeared in Sedona Journal of Emergence. The Questions are from the audience.

Greetings, all, and welcome to the loving energy I offer you today. Please relax and be receptive to me as I impart not only knowledge but also compassion and unconditional love. As we begin, let your heart come to a place of trust and openness. Take whatever time you need to do this before you continue…

Many of you have asked me recently how it is possible to hold your highest vibration, live in peace, and serve in a deeper way. Part of what I offer you today is a lesson in maintaining your purity of vibration through a balance of heart energy and of self-love. This is done through maintaining your purity of heart.

In the heart there is a connection of spirit and of your humanity. In this connection there is the balance of *matter*—the human part of you—and of *spirit*—the eternal part of you. Did you know that the human part of you is just as divine as your spirit and just as pure? There is much confusion about this.

Many of you are busy trying to prove your worthiness to those of us in spirit-form in order to receive love. We are not interested in this. It is only *you* who are proving it to yourselves. Do you think I care how many good and worthwhile things you have done? It will not change my love for you. You are good already; you are already pure.

Many of you want to ascend and serve in spirit in order to avoid some of your human experiences and human feelings. This will not do. It is only running away. Embracing your humanity will bring you closer to me. By embracing it, you are trusting that I will love you *as you are* and not as you *may be* in some future time when you have proven your worthiness or have perfected yourself. My love for you is unchangeable.

Maybe there were those around you when you were young who loved you with so many conditions attached that you felt loved only when you were *good*. Perhaps they wanted to love you but didn't know how. This not the way I, nor any other masters, guides, or others in spirit love you. So please do not try to earn what is a gift from the beginning.

Will you receive my love now as we speak? Let me hold out my hands to you so that you may receive even the touch of nurturing in the way that you need. Let me place my hands upon your shoulders and head so you know you are cared for and protected. In all times, in all situations, and in all feelings, let me be with you so that I may hold you in my heart. When I take you into my heart of hearts it is the safest and most sacred place I can offer you. In this safety of my love, you can learn to love yourself protected by my shelter.

In a way far beyond your intellect's ability to understand or process, you are now capable of loving yourself in a much higher way than ever before. To do this you must enter into the sacred place within your *own* heart where there is joy. By allowing me to show you *my* heart from the inside out you will learn to feel safe and at peace within *your* heart. Your heart is a chamber of unparalleled beauty and unfathomable depth. Yet while there is fear within you, you will not allow yourselves to probe the depths of your heart to find its loveliness.

Maybe, in its fear of being surpassed, your intellect will try to get you to return to it as a means of self-love. This is only the ego trying to compensate for the fear of feeling unlovable. Even now the intellect's inadequacy is visible. The beauty and power of the heart overrides all else and becomes your faithful haven.

Embrace more of your heart and you will find even yet more love to receive. It is what I have placed in your hearts as you have allowed me to be there. This is the love you require to fill *all* human needs. Hold your hopes high even in times of despair; know that when you go into the unexplored and dark places within yourself, there I will meet you most swiftly. As the sun is ever seeking the dark corners, so is my love ever seeking those small hurts that need tending. Rest in this assurance, and I am already there with you.

When you can receive me in this way, *I* am truly blessed with a new intimacy with *you*, which is an immeasurable gift to *my* heart. You can have no idea of how I am blessed when I can come close to you in this way. It is my deepest desire to be with you and fill whatever needs you have with love. It is a joyous reunion. Thank you ever so much for the welcoming you give me. It is the communion I have desired for so long with you.

Why do you desire communion with us when you have all of eternity to connect with the other masters?

In the amazing diversity of all life, you alone have the capability of touching and reaching a part of me that is reserved solely for connection with you. Because this part in me is reserved for you—*each of you*—no one else, master or otherwise, can touch that place and bring me communion in this way. So when you invite me into those spaces of closeness with you, the place in my own heart is no longer alone. Though I do not experience loneliness as you do, I still experience the absence that you sense when you do not feel loved. So when you allow me communion with you, you are allowing yourself to feel my love and then my gift is received and it completes a beautiful circle for me.

You see, we are not as different as you think we are. If there is a part in me that is filled by and reserved for you, then there is surely a part in you that is filled by and reserved for me. And if we are the same in this, all of the love that I hold in my being is yours as well.

There are those of you who still fear intimacy and thus cannot allow me to come too close. Intimacy has been a weapon used by others against you when you were vulnerable and open. It was not heart they wanted to share with you; it was fear. The fear, *their fear,* was so painful to you that it caused you to pull away from anyone who came later offering you union of heart. Do not mistake the love I offer you for fear. I only offer you the most positive experience of your lifetime. You must open your hearts to receive it though, and this requires trust. Trust of me and trust of yourself in making the correct choice in the correct time for you.

Can you feel your trust for this that grows? If you open your hearts to receive love, you will also begin to trust more and more. Is it not an amazing thing that to receive love when it is offered also allows you to feel more trust? That is why we in spirit say so often that if all you do is receive love for yourself then you have accomplished your purpose here. By receiving love, you create an opening to all other blessings. Then you are filled with blessings to share with others automatically! But if you try to love others without first receiving love for yourself, you drain your own precious reserves. Accept your human needs for love and companionship, and do not try to share this blessing *before* you have received it!

Do you see? It is our greatest pleasure to give you the love and blessings you desire. And if this is so, then does it not follow that we will give this to any and all who ask for it? So you see, if you receive and allow yourselves to simply be a model for others then *we* will do the work and bless the others too. In this way, it will be effortless for you all. Indeed, it is not too good to be true. Believe in miracles and they will surely unfold before you.

When you need help to open up, simply ask for more love. And if you find yourself lacking in trust or in faith then ask for that too. Yes, faith is a gift. You see, it is not something you create out of the "stuff" of third dimension. It is a gift. Receive the gift of faith and receive the love that follows it, too.

If you cannot find the trust to ask for faith, then tell us of this and we will help you still. Simply allow yourself to be *willing* to receive. *Willing* to receive it as a gift. Then we will give you the kingdom.

If you cannot trust even a tiny bit, if you cannot believe that you will be loved for who you are in this moment, if you cannot know with certainty that everything within you is already pure, just ask for this knowing to come to you, and it will. By and by, it will.

Faith is a risk, though, for many of you still. You have been let down so often. Express this to us as well and we *will* do the rest. If all this is too difficult for you or too complicated, simply *feel* the hurt and loneliness and allow me to heal it. That is trust on a very high level.

Do you already feel this love? Do you feel *my knowledge* that you are pure? You do not have to believe it. Just *feel* how much *I* believe it.

In feeling these things from me, you create healing on many bodily levels. The love you now receive as we speak goes as deep as your bones. It chases away any dark energy from the corners of your being. Nothing can hide from this light of love. You need no ceremony for this nor do you even need Archangel Michael to come in with his great sword to chase away the negativity in the darkness. Love is the great healer and accomplishes all this simply by your desire to receive it and by your willingness to be vulnerable and open.

What else shall we speak of?

I'm confused. When I listen to you speak sometimes you say "we" and sometimes you say "I." What do you mean and who is the "we" you speak of?

In my understanding, I, Mary, am one with what you would call God. In this oneness there is belonging and there is no loneliness. Because of this, I am in constant contact with Creator and all of Creation. Indeed, I could say that Creation is within me. I am the Mother of Creation. However, I alone am not the source of Creation. All of you are, too. So when I speak as "we," I speak for many other beings of love who are here with me, in oneness waiting to embrace all those of you who wish to join us. When I use the word *I*, I refer to the intimate part of me I know best as my individuality in the Oneness, the part of me that was the Mother of Jesus. I refer to the part that lived a human life and then ascended to become part of the All That Is.

Still, sharing consciousness with others allows me to *know* the truth about myself, and that is, that *I am* each of the other beings I am with. In this way *they* are also *me*. I know it must be terribly confusing to those of you who have not had a oneness experience of your own. When you do, you will know by feeling it for yourself. So for me, the *I* and the *we* are as one. In many ways they are the same.

The Oneness is an assemblage of divine beings much like yourselves, who simply wish to share their love together. In the oneness of Creation there is only one you. You uniqueness stands alone in this. But even though each of you is unique, you are not separate from love because love is what you are made of.

Just as your bodies on Earth are made up of cells, each of you is different from the other, each unique. It is like this in the fifth dimension and beyond, all beings of love sharing their beingness with each other. Source to Source, Love to Love. And in this is the hope for all humanity: The reunion of all Creation into bliss, into Oneness.

Are you ready to join the sisterhood and brotherhood of masters who walk upon the Earth? With an open heart and a desire to feel joy, nothing can stand in your way toward this goal. Be sure to remember that we are not waiting for you to perfect or purify yourselves in order for this to happen. It is only by being willing to receive love and becoming the expression of its joy that it will come to you. It will come as a gift, and that is the way you will experience it.

Move fully into your hearts and into the spaces that still hurt, and allow me to come and fill the lonely spaces. Let my heart reach into yours to show you we are not separate but one. Your heart is *now as pure as my own* in its desire to receive love! I, too, desire to receive this love. It is filling my being now, not because I am a master, not because I am perfect, but because I desire it and because I am open to it. That is all. That is the *only* requirement.

Many of you, while in your meditations, have asked me why, if you are open to receive this love, you do not feel it. It is because you want to avoid any pain associated with not having had it before. It is because you will not allow me to come in with my love and clean house! Cleaning out the old hurt sometimes takes time, and it might seem at first that it hurts more than it helps. This is always the way it is with wounds, isn't it? Especially when you have left them untended and then have become infected.

Did you know that "infected" also means "impure"? It does; look it up in your dictionaries! So what does this comparison mean? It is one of the reasons you thought in the beginning that *you* were impure! Think about it…You have old hurts, places that were not loved, and they were abandoned by you, like abandoned buildings standing alone and empty. No salves were placed upon them; no loving attention was given to them because someone else didn't love those parts of you. Because of this, you, too, decided those parts were unlovable, and you left them.

You are now still trying to leave them behind in your process toward ascension. You turn away from allowing me to see them, to love them because you believe I will also turn away from you in horror as you have been turned away from in the past, first by others, and then by yourself. Do you understand? In this process of abandoning the parts of yourself that did not receive love and attention before, *you assume* there is some part of you that is not pure!

It is only through the ignorance and fear of others that you were not loved, not because some part of you was unworthy.

Let me in to help you heal. Let me touch the places within you that have been lonely for so long: your hurts, your longings, your forgotten dreams, and your desires to be living a full and joyous life. Let me bring full and unconditional love to you as a process that will heal your life of all hurts and loneliness. But do not try to receive love into all neglected parts at once. Allow it to be gradual so that you will give yourself time to heal.

For some of you, healing will be like bringing a sleeping limb back to life. You allow in more circulation, but you do not try to stand on a foot that has been asleep for so long. You take it slow, loving and accepting yourself along the way.

When I open up to your love, I often feel sad about not having others around me in the physical. This may seem harsh, but I need human love too. Sometimes even physical contact, like hugs, helps me feel loved, or someone saying, "I love you." What about tangible signs of love to feed the human part of me?

[While Mary responds, I notice she sends out a gigantic wave of spiritual energy toward the person asking.]

This is the ultimate goal, to allow yourself to trust so completely that you will engage in loving relationships with each other across the planet. For many of you, it is indeed a matter of trust. Because of your past hurts, you have difficulty opening your hearts to one another. For some, your fear of unworthiness keeps you from receiving. For still others, the dreams of companionship you have are corrupted by your own fear of never being able to be loved by the person of your dreams. You dream wonderfully but are incapable of *believing* it will come true for you. The answer to this is not to dream less magnificently. It is to surrender your fear of never having it come true. To surrender it you only need to *feel* it. I will do the rest.

I offer my love to you at this time because it is easier for many of you to receive love from me than from another person. When you open your heart to me, it will pave the way for loving union with all others. This then will be the fulfillment you have long awaited.

Even in my ascended state, if *I* closed my heart for *one moment*, I, too, would feel alone. It is just that as I have learned about myself and understood my needs, I have come to know that I am also dependent upon love to keep me whole. I need love as much as you do, and knowing this, I keep my heart open always to receive. So you see, we are truly not different. We are all innocent *and* vulnerable, and we all need love. *It is just that I have come to accept this as a fact of my existence.* Be with me in the eternal bliss of love and open your heart.

I do want what you describe, but sometimes I am still so confused about how to open my heart, how to let go, and how to receive.

Then what you must do is feel your confusion. When things in life come that you do not understand, do not try to understand with your intelligence. Feel where the confusion is. Let it be all that you experience *without* trying to gain understanding. In feeling the confusion, you will be led to an assortment of other emotions at different times. The confusion always points to the release of the held-in emotion that limits your clarity.

So when you are confused, it is not that you are incapable of understanding with your intellect. It is that you are afraid of feeling some other emotion the light points to.

Clarity will come. Confusion is like riding a wild horse at times, is it not? Sometimes it is rough and wild and difficult to hang on. This is what it is like with unruly emotions and the confusion they bring. Often it may be appealing to just get off the horse. But the object is neither to tame the horse nor to get off it. Learn to find balance on this bucking bronco. Talk to it, and tell it to move you forward. That is the purpose of the horse. Indeed, that is the purpose of the emotions. To ride them out in their ups and downs while still maintaining your perfect balance of peace and self-trust. Then the emotions will not take you on a wild ride. You will take them for a ride. You are the master of your emotions but only if you have compassion for yourself and do not try to overly control them.

We have the greatest faith in you all. It is not an easy ride but a worthwhile one with the greatest of rewards at the end.

How does one embrace self-doubt?

Embracing self-doubt is very much like seeing the horse jumping around next to you before you have gotten up on it. You climb upon the horse anyway. You know it is the right thing to do; you have fear of doing it and yet embracing the fear you move forward with firmness. That is what it is like to embrace self-doubt. It is embracing the moment with courage, saying, "I have fear that I cannot do this but I will do it anyway and take whatever consequences come. Whatever comes from this there will be more learning for me. More learning will give me more self-love."

Is it not true that horses sense fear? Is it not also true that when you master your fear and get upon them they obey you? It is like this with confusion and other emotions. Your fear of them is greater than their power to hurt or overwhelm you. Fear is the illusion that keeps you from facing your hidden corners and learning to trust.

I, too, had fear. At times, great fear. The only way I ever defeated this fear was to trust in something greater: love. I believed that love had its own pathway toward peace, and I followed that pathway to where I am now.

Trust the love that is offered to you. Trade in your fear for the power to make yourself whole and be alone no more. Open your heart and I, we, will do the rest. This I promise. And as surely as I, Mary, was one of you once and was among you once, *I am among you now,* ready to take your hand and walk with you down the pathway of love.

Chapter 17

Let Me Be Your Comforter

This piece is my favorite channeling of Mother Mary. In it she offers such kindness, love and warmth. She reaches out to so many to offer her compassion and I have often sent copies of this to clients in need of just that. Whatever is it that hurts or makes you sad, these words are yours. It was channeled in September of 1998.

Hello my friends. It is my wish to speak with you and to ask you to invite me into your hearts for I have much to share with you. In order to receive my guidance personally, all you need do is ask and I promise I will be there.

If I can suggest a simple offering of how you can experience my presence more fully: When you sit in meditation or even in quiet contemplation place a lighted candle or a bowl of clear water in front of you, perhaps with a flower floating in it. Or simply place a piece of white paper in front of you on the table. Just an object that can hold my image so that you will have something upon which to focus, to make it easier for you to experience clearly who I am. Also this will give my essence something to settle into, almost like I am sitting next to you.

When you open your heart to receive my love and guidance, I feel as if I am invited into an open house where a beautiful table is set for me. The finest china is laid on the table and a bowl of cool water is given to me to refresh myself before I begin my repast. As I feast on the openness of your heart, let my words fill your being with the love you need. What I offer you is a new knowledge of love and how it can transform you hearts and lives.

I am a light of the world as surely as there is light in the Sun, but more everlasting is my love, for my light is not as the physical light that with each passing day goes down for the night.

My love for you is so constant that when you are in the dark night of your soul, I will come to you before you know you have need of me. I will seek you out before one tear is shed, before you can be afraid of being alone.

So let me sit with you when you are in the corner crying, your comforter pulled up tight. I will be with you. I will come under the comforter to be closer to you. For I desire to crawl into your heart and stay there. And I will bring my own blanket to warm you if you will allow me to.

Let me sneak into the quiet moments in your evenings and into the bright moments of your mornings. Let me drink your breakfast juice with you and your evening tea. And let me sit in the sun in the afternoons with you so that you are never alone.

Whenever there is a quiet time, think of receiving. Think of coming together with me in love, and I will take your hand and lead you into a garden. Is this not the peace that you all desire? It is yours; it is yours for the asking. It is all that I wish to do. It is my purpose. Do you still have doubt? Perhaps thoughts of unworthiness stop you, perhaps fear of trusting in others who say they offer love but give conditions instead. My love for you is unlike any other.

In the multitude of connections that are available to me, in the bliss and joy of all the oneness that is there for me to experience, no joy for me is greater than this: To share love with those of you who yet have doubt. Come to me now, and I will soothe all your old hurts.

Show your doubt to the light and allow your dry spirits to be refreshed; drink of the waters of peace. It is my mission to give you hope and fill your hearts to overflowing with love. Let me be your comforter. When you are lost, I will be with you in your heart of hearts. I will come to warm you in the cold places of your loneliness.

When you are confused, I will soften the frustration of your searching to allow you to see clearly what you have lost sight of. My love goes with you always to guide your footsteps lest you become afraid and wander off your chosen path. My love for you is like the willow tree that bends with the winds of storms but does not break. I will lend you my strength to allow you to continue on your journey when you are too tired to raise your head.

Most of all my love helps you to find acceptance of who you are as the source of love. Let your little child within come out to meet me and receive my gifts, for it is this part of you that can trust and find joy. Open up to that aspect of your being.

There is no part of you that is not pure, my loved ones. All that came before, in this lifetime or in the countless others before it that caused you to feel separated, is of no account. I am certain all of you can recall times of old hurts, violations, betrayals, even past mistakes, but I tell you now, they never touched you. You are as pure as *my* love is for you, and you shine with ever as much beauty. Join me in the oneness of our love together now, will you? Will you allow me to come to you and bring my own comforter in which you can curl up and find warmth? Lay you head against my breast, my child and let my words feed your spirit.

Now that you have seen how to receive love from me, let me speak for a moment about receiving love from one another. Many of you desire to receive love from those of us in Spirit and yet you shrink when receiving love from each other. It is not as easy. This is because you must trust in the same way that you trusted before when you often got hurt.

Some of you have chosen spiritual paths because in your desire to receive love it is easier to receive it from Spirit than from each other. "I have found a shortcut!" you say. Well, you have found a shortcut, but now there is a detour! You are being routed back to your original destination. It is time to face your fear of others!

I share this bit of information with you now because it will help you to ease out of the doubt. Only when you receive love from each other in human form will you truly come to terms with whatever sense of unworthiness you have about receiving unconditional love from Spirit. And if you still feel unworthy, you will not truly receive from me and others like me. Many more of you have this issue than you realize.

There are many more ways to receive love in the physical than you think. It does not have to come from family members, or from partners for that matter. It can even come from people on the street, even in a short encounter. I encourage you all to begin being as open to others as you are to your closest friends. Not that you should trust your greatest treasures to total strangers, but that you can be open in your hearts to receive from anyone who desires loving communion with you. No matter how or when that comes.

Begin to think about how in times of need there were certain people placed in your life at just the right time. It may not have been a "soul mate," as you begged for, but was it not someone who helped you grow and learn to release and receive? So prize those moments that you remember as being difficult. Prize those moments that you remember not receiving what you *wanted* but were, instead, given what you *needed*, what helped you grow toward love. These were the precise times that we were with you when you could not see us. Remembering those times will help you to see that even when you thought had abandoned, we were there. In times of trouble or stress when you don't feel our loving arms around you, we are with you nonetheless.

This is how our love is for you. We desire not to take credit for giving you what you always want, but only desire to see that you receive what you need. Even if for a time it means that you don't see us in the process. Even if it means you doubt us and pull away in mistrust and fear. Though we may miss your presence in communion, we know that in the long run, by giving what you need, you will be at peace.

At this time in many of your lives receiving from each other will help you open more to my love and the love of countless others in Spirit. It will be like coming full circle to understand of the nature of love.

Many of you often wear masks that say, "I'm fine, I am *all right*. Am I not smiling?" but inwardly you are hurting the hurts of years of loneliness. Why is it so difficult for you to let yourselves be vulnerable? Are you afraid of being hurt all over again? Opening up to your feelings is the only way you can come to a place of peace. When you need to share feelings, look around you and see the person we have placed in your life for you to talk to. Speak of your pain, and let me lift it for you.

When you hide your feelings from others, you hide from your own nature and cannot come into communion with who you are in Spirit. This is an act of denying self-love. When you hide your self-love in this way, you change who you are. Even others who *wish* to give you love no longer recognize you. It is then that you feel most alone because you have pulled away from yourself.

Then many of you go even one step further and pretend that no one else loves you, either. And believing this, you think you must hide further because if others do not love you, then it is not acceptable to be around them. Having convinced yourself of the truth of all of this, you feel unworthiness and pull away from all who could give you love, especially me.

Often others will see the pain beneath your smile. They see your hurt even when you will not acknowledge it. This is what it means to be unconscious: pretending you are happy and pretending others do not see the truth about you. So do not hide your sad face behind a mask that says,

"I am fine." Expose your feelings to others and to me, so you can receive the love and healing we so long to give you. Take my comfort and wrap yourself in it for as long as you have need of it. It is truly my greatest joy to give you this.

Now, if there is a question or two on any subject, please ask."

I have a question about diet. I am used to drinking beverages like coffee that contain caffeine, and I suppose this is not good for me. Could you help me understand why I seem to have a dependence upon it and maybe how I can reduce my intake of it?"

Very good, thank you. Many millions of people have this same question, so it is good to give you the information. Let me first describe how caffeine affects the brain and body.

When you drink coffee and other beverages that contain caffeine your body experiences an artificial "high." Caffeine attaches itself to the same receptor sites in the brain that natural endorphins do. This then tells the brain that it does not need any more endorphins and the brain quits producing them. The natural joy-giving endorphins are blocked from production when you drink caffeine. You are substituting the natural, healing, joyful endorphins for a chemical compound.

After daily use of caffeine for an extended period, the brain shuts down production of endorphins. Even after a day or two of discontinuing your use of caffeine, your body does not produce them. It is as if the brain, believing the artificial stimulants will always be supplied, thinks natural ones are no longer necessary. Your body, then needing its natural chemicals and finding none, resorts to demanding the artificial ones. This is how the addition syndrome starts.

Take heart, however, if you can resist the urge for caffeine for a week, in some cases less, the brain, lacking its endorphins for an extended period starts up its production of them once more. The body was designed to experience ongoing joy, and endorphins are just one of the many ways for you to find bliss even in third dimension. Do not rob yourself of this joy by finding a cheap substitute.

Sadly, this is the story with sugar, too. It affects the body in a similar chemical way and robs you of natural ways of feeling bliss. Artificial chemicals produce joy that is not joy, but deprivation. Perhaps now it will be easier for all of you to abstain from these things. Now you have the reassurance that when your body comes back to normal, the brain will once again produce the natural joy chemicals. Unfortunately, the stronger the drugs and the longer the period used, the longer it takes the body to bounce back.

The brain was created to give you all the peaceful sense of well being you deserve. It makes sense does it not? Perhaps knowing this will make it easier for you to find balance. Let the brain return to its normal function; give yourself a week or two to see the difference.

We were speaking earlier of sharing love with each other. Food is a wonderful thing to share. When you share a meal with someone, gathering together to nurture your bodies, you also nurture your spirits. Wherever people are gathered together there is nurturing.

Being together while you are eating is a wonderful thing. You allow your body to obtain what it needs because you are obtaining what your spirit needs as well. In this way you do not eat for brain joy, but for bodily nourishment. Your brain, being washed in the natural chemicals it needs by your being in communion with others, will allow your body to select foods that are appropriate for it. Do you see?

Have you not been told of how "being in love" creates many wonderful and blissful chemicals in the brain? It is true, when you allow yourself to receive love it is a joyful experience on many levels of body, mind, and spirit. Many of you already know that the substance chocolate can produce an artificial chemical reaction similar to being in love. Chocolate is simply caffeine and sugar. Now you know the true story. Come together in loving interaction, I tell you; nourish yourselves in the most natural way designed. Thank you for asking about this.

In all of these things, the aspect of trust comes in once more doesn't it? "If I refrain from chemicals, do I trust my body to produce its own?" Going through withdrawal, as you call it, is your period of trust. Trust yourself in all things. Trust your body, who loves you more than you can imagine. Has it not served you all these years, in spite of how you have treated it?

When you trust your body to readjust itself to a healthy balance, you then free yourself to find peace within your mind and spirit. Trust all parts of yourself to find this balance as well. Balance of mind, body, and spirit can only be found through self-examination and self-trust.

Self-trust is not an easy thing to accomplish. It is found, of course, within the heart. When you come to that place in your journey of finding self-trust you will also find empowerment. This is the source of your power: self-trust. Knowing who you are in your spirit, trusting that spirit to be pure, divine, and holy is the greatest act of self-trust you can make. When you find this place, you will have found peace.

The peace brought about by the empowerment of self-trust is the single greatest force next to self-love that you can have within. So you see, learning to love all that is within you, your sadness, your fear, your vulnerability, leads you to self-trust.

Self-trust is ultimately your own internal guidance system. Though many people will tell you what is right for you, only you can know your own heart. Your heart, your feelings, your spirit are yours alone. Come to see that there is nothing inside of you that is not immaculate and innocent and you will have found your True Self.

Let me be your guide in this glorious exploration. It is my joy to love you now in ways you will ultimately love yourself. In the unconditional acceptance of your many traits, gifts, and even foibles, you will come to know the unparalleled beauty of who you are. You are already perfect my children, already spotless and so loved by the divine, the one you call God and Spirit.

Let us embrace. Let us be as one. Let us find peace together, and I will show you your beauty. Open your heart and receive my love.

Chapter 18

Kwan Yin and the Open Heart

This beloved master worshipped by many around the world is not someone I have channeled frequently, though when I do I am filled to overflowing with a loving energy akin to that of Mother Mary. Different in many ways from each other their energy seems to emanate from a similar place in Source and they always touch people in a deeply emotional and profoundly loving and personal way.

There is another attribute they also share, a deep devotion to those of us on Earth. In a uniquely feminine way, Kwan Yin compels each person to receive more love than they even know they can handle or receive. I saw this done most recently during a weekend retreat I held in another state.

Toward the end of my time with the people attending the retreat I had the opportunity to channel Kwan Yin as a request from one of the attendees. I had just finished channeling Djwal Khul who was speaking of how love as we know it is not the same as the love they offer us. He told us how true unconditional love is unfathomable, unknowable. I had heard of this before, even sensed what it approached but could not in my limited way even begin to grasp it. It was only later that we, as a group, were treated to an understanding, indeed an experience, of just what D.K. told us about.

As I prepared for the last channeling of the weekend, I relaxed and was told by the masters that Kwan Yin would be next to come through. I readied myself for her gentle words. As she came into my body, I felt something I had not felt before: I had automatically gone to a greater distance from my own emotions and body. It was as if I was lifted up to a place where I was beyond feeling what was to be said. Only later did I fully realize why.

Kwan Yin spoke to the group, greeting everyone cordially with her characteristic flow of love and grace. She asked for the person who requested her to speak to come and sit before her. I had often seen the masters do this in group, offer a single individual healing or love that pertained to many, or all, in the audience. Kwan Yin took this man's hands in hers and began to speak.

The words that flowed from her were the most beautiful I have ever channeled. It was pure poetry. She began by saying how she was honored and even humbled to be asked for from one so dedicated to Spirit. She told him how she had served many now in the Earth plane but how his devotion was rare in her experience. She poured out such love as I have never seen or felt before. Her expression to this man was exactly the expression of the words Djwal Khul had taught us about only moments before. It was the unlimited expression of unconditional and unknowable love. As I spoke I felt like Shakespeare must have felt when writing his love sonnets. It was as glorious and stunning an expression of love as I have ever heard.

As she continued to speak I felt myself drawn into the exchange with the man before her. It was as if I *was* Kwan Yin speaking the words. This was a different joining than I had felt with Mary or with the other guides. I felt none of my own emotions, or were mine so inseparable from hers I could not tell the difference? I do not know. I only know as I sat there being her vessel, she spoke the words that expressed with loving gratitude a communion of love between two beings that only begins to express the unknowable and unfathomable love we will someday come to know and to be. When she was done, there was not a dry eye in the room.

Usually I am also touched in my emotions by what is said, but that was not the case that day. I returned to my body and found everyone sitting back in silence holding tissues in their hands and dabbing their eyes. There was a peace that filled the room that was palpable, and everyone was content and filled.

I am certain I was able to bring through that particular message only because I had become so removed from my own feelings. Days later, after I returned from the workshop, I meditated on what transpired that day in group and felt the feelings of love return. I, too, had to reach for a tissue or two as I finally felt what everyone else in the room had felt. A knowing of what love is, a glimpse of what is to come. It was magnificent. It was unspeakable.

I know it was no coincidence that I did not have my tape recorder running for that session. The personal connection that was made between the man who sat before Kwan Yin that day and the rest of the group was for them only. I thought about this later and knew it would have almost violated the intimacy of the exchange. It was not something that could have been rendered here anyway, without having heard all that came before and feeling the energy in the room of all those present.

I found a new respect for Kwan Yin that day and yet still know I see only a tiny part of what she is. I know she and I will join again in this way, and it is a time I look toward with much joy and anticipation.

Though the following piece I offer of Kwan Yin's is not the poetry of that retreat weekend, it still shows how loving and kind her words can be, as well as enlightening. It was channeled in April of 2000 and appeared in the *Sedona Journal of Emergence* just as it appears here.

Experiencing Self-Love through the Open Heart.

Hello, Beloved Ones. It is good to be with you all today. I have heard from many of you recently about your continued struggles with the healing of the emotional body. In the higher realms there is constant connection with emotion as we interact with third dimension but for many of you it is indeed difficult to stay connected with your feeling center, especially when there is still pain to be experienced and released. It is often easier to alternately feel, think, feel and think without staying in your heart to feel at all times.

When you desire to experience self-love and the healing it brings you in an ongoing way, it is important to stay in the heart. Many of you, when in distress, often consult the intellect in order to gain strength, find hope and feel relief from the pain. There is wisdom in gaining a sense of strength but do not go to the empty pot of the intellect for what is to be found in the fountain of faith. The heart is the center of that faith.

Life is full of many choices. When choices are presented to you, it is not yet automatic for many of you to consult the heart for decision making. Whatever is in your path, use your heart only to decide. Use your head for common sense decisions, of course, like what to have for dinner, or which gasoline to put in your car. Use your heart to show you how it will feel to embrace a path that is presented to you. If you find you cannot locate your heart for consultation, it means there is something in the way. Then is the time for healing.

As a test of whether you are in your heart: try feeling my energy now... It will surely come through the written word because I have decreed it to do so. In my world of the ascended realms, this is an easy thing to do. It is so because I surround everything I do with love from my open heart. It is not the same as making an intent. There is much confusion for most of you about this. An intent is not a consultation of the intellect, it is an *act* of the heart. It is something that must be felt, not thought. Feel then my intent to send you love through this article. Go to your heart to do this.

As you open your heart to feel my love, you will notice a barrier. Most of you have this. It is a barrier to block painful experiences from coming into your aura. In the process of blocking pain, you also block love from those of us from "above." We are not better than you, of course, just more experienced in opening ourselves to All That Is. When you encounter this barrier, slow down and ask yourselves, "Where did I deviate from my path? How can I let go of control to now receive that which I desire?" Let the answers flow into your consciousness. Do not try to reason them out. Above all do not try to do this without our help. Come to us in meditation for assistance.

Whatever thoughts or answers come, do not analyze them or try to change yourself. Do not struggle to think about things and arrive at the right conclusion. That is the old way of effort. Allow this process to be effortless. That is the way of love. It is the way of receiving, and receiving is what you are here to do today. Today is the day I have come to give you the gift of peace. Let the knowledge simply flow through you, showing you once again where to connect with your feelings. When you can feel the images, unite with them; that is where the healing is. That is where the truth is.

As you let go of the old patterns of defenses, resentments, judgments, and anger, you will notice a significantly lighter feeling surrounding and filling your heart. This does not mean that all your old hurts have gone. It is only that you have now received the reassurance and support you asked for in order to move ahead and heal the old hurts. It is the confidence of faith—the knowing of my presence, and the presence of others around you, giving you love—that will sustain you in your desire to move ahead to embrace love.

As you move on and face your fears and hurts, we are with you. We are loving you. We are one. We, too, will feel your hurt with you and help you let go and heal. Did you know it was not your job alone to let go? Of course not. We would never ask you to do this alone. It is what others in your world tell you that you must do. Those others have no idea of the power of our love. No, we ask only that you are willing to give up your desire to do things alone. It is the ego only that will tell you that you cannot get the "credit" for winning if you do not go through the hardship by yourself. Where is the credit or the gain in being in pain?

I ask you, why *would* you want to do this alone? Is it the fear that if you ask for help, it will not be there? Why would we tell you to lean on us and then abandon you? I tell you, we could not! It is not in our make-up to do so. We were not created that way. Let go then of your burden and receive our help. Relax into love and into harmony. Let this peace fill your heart and surrender to the naked knowledge that you are loved—unabashedly, unreservedly. Wholly and completely you are loved. Let us nurture you. We have ways of giving to you that you cannot imagine. The simplest way I can show you this is to tell you, let us love you as you are. You do not need to change a hair on your head. You are perfect already.

Each choice in your life will stimulate a feeling in your heart center. At times, the feelings stimulated will show you old patterns of fear or old patterns of interaction that do not serve you. When this occurs, move into the heart space fully to embrace the feeling stirring there. Though there be pain or fear, there is also faith, joy and love. All these things your heart contains at once. Let your heart be your guide as the opening process gently gains momentum. Let it flow and be one with us. Let our love flow into you as if it were beautiful music entering your ears and filling your being with joy. It is effortless to listen to music; let it be effortless to fill your body with love.

Moving into the heart space fully is a way of being. *Begin to organize your life around a state of being.* You will gain nothing by occupying yourself with empty activities when you are in fear or pain. These things fill your time but do not fill your heart and rob you of joy. They are only a temporarily distraction from your true state of affairs within. Go to your heart now and rest. Find the peace that is there for you, the peace that is at the core of you. The peace that tells you that you are loved.

Imagine yourself in a serene place. Breathe in fully, and enjoy the state of grace that is offered to you from above. Visualize with me now a beach, the mountains, or a simple chair in the middle of a beautiful garden. Breathe in fully the scents that surround you there. Relax your body and your mind. Let time pass.

Let all of your affairs now flow from this center of ease. Begin now to change the way you order your life. Reset your priorities to allow for love, for contentment, the calm you have always wanted to feel. I ask you now: *What is worth doing if it does not fill you with peace?* When you are in distress and without joy, ask yourself, "Is this the way I want to spend my life?" Ask your heart this question, and the answer may surprise you. Go deep within to find the answer.

When you seek joy, it is yours to create with us. the joy you have always wanted to feel is in this garden of co-creation. Let the burdens you have carried for so long fall away from you now. It is time to relax every limb and surrender all old ideas and live in peace. The harmony you have long awaited has come. Let it flow into you heart, now emptied of fears, empty except for love.

Receive a feeling of peace as it flows in your direction. Be one with all that is around you. Be one with me as I offer you direction and guidance. Be with me now that I am with you, offering you my love. Surrender your ideas of what will allow you to receive love and peace. Surrender your old ideas of what you must do to receive love. There is nothing to do, nothing to think about, nothing to change about yourself. You are perfect. You are beautiful. You are the divine creation of a Master of Love. All is in perfection. As we reside together in this peace, let me now share with you these simple truths.

Visualize yourself as a circle. In the center of the circle is the heart. On the edge of the circle there are many things: time, the intellect, possessions, other people and their ideas, your job, your concerns. Outside of the circle are your fears. Your fears are not truly a part of you. They can only enter the circle through the intellect. Once connected with the intellect, they can affect your choices. The most important choice they affect is where you place you focus of attention.

The goal of fear is to convince you to disconnect from your heart. If you escape fear by going to your intellect, then fear has succeeded. Love is to be found in the heart not the intellect. It is where your divine connection lies. It is where your joy is. It is where peace is to be found. Certainly peace is not to be found in the mind. The mind is like a restless kitten always jumping, running, ever distracted. The heart is where the kitten sleeps, in peace, in contentment, in the knowledge and safety of love.

As you move toward the heart, you move toward the center of your life. It allows you to experience all things in the circle while still being connected to the divine, to love. Here, you will experience self-love and contentment by being in the center. Do not worry about what lies outside of love, or outside of the center of who you are. As long as you are in the heart all that you experience in life is encompassed by love. This is what it means to be centered in your life.

When you spend so much of your time in the intellect, you often subject yourself to the fears that lurk next to you on the outside of the circle. You are in danger of living in fear most of the time. Fear is aware of this and encourages you to come close by living in your head. This way, fear can easily attach to you and affect your life and decisions, moving you away from your heart and from love, moving you away from your power. Surely you know by now that the only power you can wield in this world or any other is the power of love, the power that is in your heart. This is true power. It is the power to change lives, yours and others.

So how do you place yourself in the center of life? Place yourself in the center of your heart and experience life from the perspective of love. Allow your goal to be centered on feeling peace. When you feel no peace, reorder your life and move once again to the center. Do this as many times as is necessary to gain a long lasting sense of harmony. It does not matter how many times you have to readjust your life or your choices to remain in the center of love and of harmony. What matters only is the desire to do so, and you will surely succeed.

Remember you are not going through this alone. We are with you every step of the way. But we cannot make choices for you. When you make choices to stay away from peace, for whatever reason, we will never force you to go back. We will never force you to do anything. That is not love. We will always honor your choices.

If you remember only one thing from my words here, remember this. Ask yourself often: Why am I doing something that does not allow me to feel peace today? There is nothing more important than this. There are always reasons to put off the decision to reorder your life: children, spouses, jobs, moneys owed, the list is infinite. There is nothing you cannot do if you desire to do it. Our help is with you at all times, our love is more constant than the Sun, more true that the North Star, more full than the full moon at it's monthly zenith. All this and more we have to offer you.

Come to us often with what you desire to do, even though it seems to you impossible. Impossible is our specialty! That is what we do best. When you surrender, trying to do things on your own, it will come. Whatever your desire is, it will come. Perhaps while you are sleeping we will bless you as we bless the innocent babe. With every breath we will breathe love into you.

You are the innocent babe in our universe. It is you to whom we desire to give the world. It is you we love. Not your neighbor, not the gifted and shining ones of the world who make much of their own accomplishments, but you. You are our gifted one, our very own child of light. Allow us to give you the world. Simply ask us to help you live in peace, and it will be so. We have no empty promises, only love to give. It is our word we offer you. Believe it wholeheartedly. Was it not said, "God spoke and there was light." It is this very same word we give you, the gift of light, the gift of love. You are our holy child; we are powerless to give you anything but the best of our love.

Please live in peace, my beautiful ones. We exist to bless you.

Chapter 19

Moccasin

Moccasin first came to me as a spokesperson for the Council of Elders, a group of masters from native tribes around over the world. She was humble, patient and insistent. I could not say no. Her energy was as golden as the grain of the Great Plains. She was loving, understanding and powerful in a way that instantly endeared her to me. She was a member of one of the Plains tribes from North America, as I had been in numerous past lives.

Moccasin's presence feels to me inseparable from the Earth's. To unite with her is to also unite with Earth in as profound a way as I have ever experienced. Her presence defies description, and I sense she hovers just above my conscious perception, ever leading me to become fully who I am and join with her. If I do not unite fully with myself beyond ego and intellect, I know I will not completely know her or the other Elders.

I have often viewed the process of channeling like seeing my body as a bottle that fills up with fluid and then tips over to pour out its contents onto those who are listening. This metaphor has never been more accurate than when I am with Moccasin and the Council. The first few times I channeled them, it was difficult for me to hold the energy without feeling overloaded.

Channeling Moccasin brings me to a place where I can feel the soil beneath my feet, smell the breeze that sweeps across my face, and watch the waters flowing past me as I gaze up into the mountains drawing strength and courage. When I feel these things, I know I am looking through her eyes. All I have to do is stay in this image, breathe deeply, and allow her to be with me. When she comes to me, it is always with her full power of spirit. I am in awe of her even though I yet glimpse only a tiny part of who she is.

I first received information from Moccasin and the Council of Elders, when I was at the home of some close friends, Candy and Ron. This is a couple I met while holding regular meditation groups at my office in Kalispell. They were by no means beginners to meditation or to other aspects of spirituality, so even at our first meeting we had lots in common. It was because of these similarities and shared experiences in the world of spirit that we quickly became friends. In the months to come, our relationship grew into a deep friendship that was later to grow into a loving bond between the three of us that seemed to have its roots in some other time we had all know each other. We all felt this connection along with gratitude to have connected again in this lifetime.

In the early '90s, I began been holding channeling groups at their house, which was an hour or so away from where I lived, and the response was good from people in their area. One night, I drove down to have dinner with Candy and Ron and to hold a channeling session at their house. We finished with dinner, sitting around the dining room table before the others arrived when Candy asked me the question that was to begin my relationship with the Council. Neither of us knew then that it would grow into the relationship that has become so powerful for us.

As the dinner dishes were cleared away and we were relaxing together, Candy posed the fateful question.

"Do you ever get impressions from objects?" she asked me.

"No, I'm usually not very good at psychometry," I replied, "Must not be one of my psychic gifts."

"Well, I was just wondering because I have some stones from my grandmother who grew up on the east side,"—the East side of the continental divide, in the Rocky Mountains of Montana—"and I thought maybe you could get some impressions or something from them."

Candy's grandmother was a teacher in a one-room schoolhouse in the plains of Montana in the first part of the last century. She lived with her family and worked on land that, not too many years before, was the homeland of one of the native prairie tribes.

"Okay, I guess it wouldn't hurt to try," I said.

Candy got the items out of a box and handed them to me.

As she placed the items in my hand, I could see the "stones" were not ordinary rocks but stone implements of some kind—rocks fashioned into tools. They appeared to be made of a granite-like stone, worn smooth in places. One looked like a mano, the Spanish word for a hand-held stone tool used for grinding corn. It was flat, rectangular and about an inch and a half thick with an indentation alongside one edge for gripping. The other edge was smooth and rounded. The next stone was rounded and smooth, somewhat egg-shaped; its use was not as easily deduced. And finally, the last stone was roughly triangular and looked as if it had been attached to a stick because there were marks along its surface that looked like it was rubbed smooth by leather or some other kind of straps.

As Candy placed the smooth stones in my hands, to my amazement and delight I was instantly filled with a sensation of vast spaces and open skies. I saw in my mind a picture of golden fields and grasses waving in the wind as the prairie opened up before me.

"I can feel this!" I exclaimed. "What a wonderful sensation of freedom this gives me. I feel as if I am in a vast prairie walking or floating among the sweet grass, open fields, and blue skies, and the sky is so vast! I feel like

I am in a tribe of the native peoples who are united with the land and are very peaceful."

I continued to get impressions from holding the stones. A complete picture of early native prairie life opened up within me. I felt as if I was being privy to another time, a time when life was simple, pure and heart-centered.

"I'm getting a feeling of being part of the Earth, of being valued, cared for and protected by her. It's as if there's a deep richness within my being and within hers that we share, a feeling of valuing each other, a sense of communing. Yes, it's a deep sense of knowing that, at some point, some place, we are one. I feel centered, empowered and free all at once. It's as if I know who I am and understand my place in the universe, and accept it is here on the Earth, with my people around me. My life, dignity, and place of contentment is assured. Everything is so peaceful."

I continued to get more impressions about the tribes there. Deeper intuition and sensations kept coming to me, so I continued to describe to Candy and Ron what I saw and felt.

"It feels like the tribes back then didn't want anything to do with fighting the white man. They were willing to share their love for the Earth and all she had to give, but were pushed so far they could only fight back in confusion and bewilderment as a last resort, not understanding why the white man wanted *all* there was to have of the land. There is a deep sense of wanting to share what the Earth has to give with everyone so all can come into this peace.

"I can sense what the people felt about each other then, too. It's as if I am in the midst of a large gathering where everyone has a job and a purpose. There is laughter and productivity, but not in the way we know it now. It's all about balance and joy. The laughter I'm feeling is pervasive. It permeates all their activities. There is also a profound lack of stress. It's incredible."

I yearned to go deeper into the experience and feel more of the impressions. In fact, I felt a longing to be there in the harmony I felt. "It was so peaceful," I could only say, as tears came to Candy's eyes and she could sense the feelings I was getting, understanding the richness and meaning of life back then by hearing my words.

We sat in silence for a few moments, all of us feeling the reverie that was created by the connection with the stones and the flow of information. I felt such a quiet ebullience about life, sensing what it meant to be alive in those times. I could only marvel at the feelings of simplicity and calm that remained within. We decided to wait for further information until group time so everyone could share in this unique experience. I hoped it would be as peaceful and as powerful.

The other attendees for the channeling session arrived shortly and we all got settled into a circle in Candy and Ron's living room. For the first half of our evening interaction, I channeled my usual motley crew of ascended masters, Archangel Michael, Kuthumi, and others. We took a break and after coming back to group, a new energy approached me. It was Moccasin. She didn't announce herself by name that night, but I knew it was the same energy I had felt earlier. She seemed to me to be a being that was earthy, mysterious and wise. Mysterious perhaps because I couldn't yet grasp even half of her energy.

She spoke for her people, a tribe of the plains—I didn't know which one—and for other native peoples of Earth, who I would later come to know as the Council of Elders. I felt riveted to my own internal center and appeared to be in the midst of what I can only call grace. They identified themselves simply as the "Native Old Ones." Their power was definitely understated, and I knew they held great wisdom. I was glad I could share these energies with all who had showed up for the channeling.

As I surrendered to receive the guidance and words I was to give the group that night, I felt a hint of Moccasin's powerful being fill me up. So much so that found myself gripping the edge of my wooden chair and holding for dear life as she came to me. She, as spokesperson for the "Old Ones" had this to say:

"We have come to speak of the stories that will begin again, tales that will not originate from the Old Ones such as us, but the tales that will come from you. They are the stories that will come from the *heart* that you will feel yourselves begin to connect with as you bind yourselves firmly to the energy within your own heart spaces.

"These will be the tales of your own lives and of your origins. They will be stories of your journeys from distant places and stories of your many lifetimes lived on this planet. It will be an incorporation of history and wisdom. Its purpose will be to begin to tell the story of the Earth. It will be the story of what you know of as the "New Earth," the Earth as she will be when once again reunited with her peoples, *all her peoples*, red, black, yellow, white, all people. It is the time of the rainbow peoples, the rainbow tribes. These stories will include information before the birth of the New Earth, with its surrounding loving energy and in conjunction with its beginning. The tales will begin now because this *is* the beginning, the time of conception, the time of going within to nurture the singing spirit voice being formed.

"So we, the Old Ones, have come not to aid you in finding your voice, but to encourage you to begin your search for it. Acknowledge who you are. Respond to that part of you that yearns for spirit contact in your life. The Earth herself has been calling to you. Wake up and remember who you are. You are a child of Spirit, born to be free, to know the oneness that is your heritage, to know the peace that is a part of who you are

"Your song is there in your breast, feel it and sing it aloud. Others will hear it and remember their own songs, too. Soon there will be a joyous harmony heard by all peoples. All will attune themselves to it. Within the space of a year and a half, the Earth herself will awaken and begin sending out an essence from her own core that will resonate in vibrational harmony with your own melody. It will be heard by all: loud, but not discordant, joyful and vibrant for all who wish to join in.

"Let the dances begin, for Earth herself has a new body, one of joyous light and with a new connection with her people. It is Earth herself that rejoices now, for in the coming years ahead there will be times of such great joy that the old bodies we exchanged for our bodies of light would have fallen by the wayside. They could not have contained such a great magnitude of light.

"Our physical bodies will not turn to dust as you were once told. They will instead resonate with a joyous sound themselves as the shedding of the old skin gives way to the new more complete fabric of that reality we call love. This is not love not as you once knew it, sparse and rare, but love as *we* knew it then and still know it now, vibrant and singing, unlimited in its scope, unable to be measured. It is this we call Great Mystery, the unfathomable love of Spirit and Earth for all her peoples, for her one people that are made up of all tribes.

"This love we speak of is in the air that you breathe, the waters with which you refresh yourselves and drink. It is *everything* that you are now and will be forever. Imagine that: forever, lasting and joyous! So sing! Sing your songs of gratitude, of new beginnings, and with Earth celebrate the coming time of change.

"In the times to come there will be those present on Earth who did not know of the hardships you have endured to get to where you are now. The hardships, that in times to come you will laugh about. You will sing songs about the "mistakes" that have been made—mistakes that do not have their meanings in judgment, but only in awareness. In the heart's understanding of love there is *only* awareness, there is no right or wrong. There is only love."

When the Elders spoke through me to the others present the group became hushed. You could have heard a pin drop. Still about this time a few sniffles were heard, as people teared-up at the beauty of the words being spoken. The Elders continued:

"These are the songs that you will write, the songs that you will sing. They will simply come from your heart; they will not come from the brain so do not "try" to construct them in your intellect first. The connection with them comes in dreamtime; it comes in meditation times. It comes in the times of singing to your children when there are no words, the moment before you start to sing. It is the love you feel that will form the words. Trust and it will be there, effortless and flowing. Dream your dreams of hope and peace; that is where you will find your song.

"This small part of our wisdom is what we have come to share with you. This planet is one of such beneficence and rare inner beauty. She has given us life with abundance and purpose while we were here, and even now while we are with her in spirit. Many of us will return again to honor her in physical form, the planet that gave us life so long ago. But we await a time when we can join with her and celebrate her new beginning in peace and in joining with others who have remembered who they are and wish to dance with us and celebrate the joyous harmony of light and fellowship.

"So take care in this period of birth not just for Earth but for yourselves. Care very much for yourselves; receive as much as you can. You are loved so greatly by Earth herself. This does not even begin to include the energies that come from beyond, the energies that come from within, or from other places in the universe. If you were but to feel the love that Earth has for you, you would ponder how you could spend all of your days upon her surface and yet be able to contain what she has to give you. It is in seeking her fulfillment that she gives this to you. Receive it as the gift she gives.

"Continue to allow your roots to go deep. To connect with her and receive from her. Allow your hearts to be so full that the words will spill over and become the gifts you give to teach others to connect with her as well. It will help them find their way home; it will help them remember who they are. It is only this that Earth desires of you in return for her love. Even so, were you not to sing and pass along the living joy of love, she would give it to you anyway.

"Why we have come, why we are here is the same reason that all of you are here. To feel the living love of Earth in connection with her spirit, to reconnect and through that love, allow others to connect as well.

"The holiday of Thanksgiving celebrated in the fall on this continent was but a shadow image of what we felt every day. The early settlers did not understand this. We could not fully participate in their holiday because of this and they thought us ungrateful. This could not have been further from the truth. Our joy in receiving from Earth was vast and complete. We did not wait a year to give thanks but honored her every day we were alive, feeling blessed to be on her surface and commune with her.

"The plants and animals participated in this celebration of life, having knowledge of the full cycle of life. The full cycle of life in spirit is so complete that it mattered not what form life took. It could be life of the waters, life of the Earth; life continued always. Death was not feared, but was honored as a new beginning. A gateway to other places where only those in spirit could go. Though we may have felt momentary loss of companionship when those of us passed on to the spirit realm, we knew the connection would endure from time to eternal time. It was not considered important when we would connect again, whether in physical space or that of spirit. What mattered was to be fully present at each moment of life we were in, to be fully alive and aware.

"We had no concept of death as you know it, so sure were we of life beyond the physical. We were so certain of life in the spirit world that we had contact with it daily. We "saw" many of our elders having peaceful gatherings. We feared not for them or for ourselves. Birth and death are but the same process, a part of the life cycle to be enjoyed and continued. There are no endings, no separation, just being.

"There are many beings with you at all times, many more than any of you have awareness of: loved ones, guides, angelic beings, many beings—as many as you can imagine and still more. Allow yourselves to discern their existence with you, and you will benefit beyond measure. Feel your heart, your own spirit, and you will allow them to come very near to you. Choose to allow them to connect with you and they will, most easily. Do not mistake a sudden impulse to think about something as coincidence. Do not pass off as coincidence any occurrences in your awareness when you open yourselves up such as this. There *are* no coincidences, no mistakes of sight. When you ask for connection, it is simply given to you. Trust, and know this will happen.

Guide your own hearts to this place of peace that we speak of. Let your songs be heard and open to the miracle of life. Live each day. Love others each time the sun rises and be grateful for all that is around you each time the moon passes in its cycle. Live fully and feel the freedom of life as Earth blesses you with her abundance. Be grateful for your lives. It is this we have come to share with you."

After they finished speaking everyone in the audience was quiet. I sensed they were feeling the same calm I had after my first meeting with Moccasin. During the delivery of the message there were often tears in the eyes of those present and the box of tissues had been passed around the circle. I had learned early on in giving group channeling sessions to have plenty of tissues on hand. The peace that filled the air assured me all was well with those in attendance.

After group, on my drive home, I began exploring my own perceptions of who these wise beings were and what was to be my relationship with them. It seems there were a number of individuals present in the group of Old Ones. The beings in the group were so closely connected with one another that, although I knew this group to be made up of several individuals, it was hard for me to tell distinct and different personalities; there was a togetherness and a oneness they shared. They also radiated a serene toughness that spoke of the binding spirit of the group. They were resilient to the core. What came through most strongly was a feminine energy. The members of the group seemed to be both male and female, though the overriding feeling I had was one of an almost androgynous energy.

I could feel a strong and deep sense of love emanating from them, and, at the same time, the gentle toughness they exuded would not mince words. Their message of honoring Earth in the highest way possible touched me deeply. It was a message of humility, one of taking responsibility for who we are and what we do at all times and ultimately, being responsible for knowing who we are and for being who we are. If I was to channel them again, I knew I would be hearing more about this business of responsibility for who we are.

I felt strongly that they still walk among us, though now in spirit, and are eminently more able to guide us through the remaining years of this period in our history. In the future, they were indeed to speak more of the transformation to come for us all and how we are to prepare for the changes. I knew this message and its wisdom was one I had come into this lifetime to learn and pass along to others, helping people to understand that a joining of all peoples into a peaceful way of life can only enhance who we are as individuals. I felt, or maybe hoped, that I was beginning to become part of the oneness they spoke of. I finished my drive home through the tall pine trees and the quiet with a renewed sense of optimism and a peaceful heart.

Chapter 20

The New Ghost Dance

In the latter part of the 1800s, as the decimation of the native Indian tribes and their cultures was occurring in North America, several groups of Indian tribes banded together to entreat Great Spirit to come to their aid. They danced what was then called the Ghost Dance. It was a formal and sacred dance to ask for the return of the buffalo and the banishment of the white people so they could return to their way of life unmolested. On the surface it appears not to have succeeded.

What really happened though in this interchange between native peoples and the entity that they call Great Spirit? Did God abandon them? I don't think so. All one has to do is look at the resurgence of indigenous cultures in our emerging New Age. As we progress toward an uncertain future, we must learn from the past. In our history lie the answers, and we are finally coming around to see what was almost lost in our ignorance.

The Council of Elders speaks to me often of what they call the New Ghost Dance. It is a dance, they say, that will include all peoples around the world and exclude no one. It is the worldwide dance of peace. In channeling an historical Sioux leader named Red Cloud and other Elders in the Council, I have learned much. What the Council insists upon is a peace that brings together all peoples in a divine harmony that is all-inclusive. "It is the dance of peace whose time has come," they say. Some call this the time of the Rainbow Tribes. Perhaps it is not by way of an answered prayer from so long ago that this occurs, but who knows? How many of us have prayed for things that do not come to pass, only to see that what we receive is better than what we ask for? Who knows what Great Spirit has in mind for all of its people or how it works in a way that leaves human understanding far behind.

The slaughter of innocent peoples and the destruction, or attempted destruction, of their cultures is something that saddens me deeply. Nothing we do or say can make up for the losses, or change the bloody slaughter, of those times. In my understanding it was simply wrong, unspeakably so. What we can do now is learn to treat each other with respect, acceptance, and unity as we approach a planetary population that is taxing not only our resources but also our understanding of where to look for guidance, balance, and harmony.

In my work with individuals of varied backgrounds and races, I have come to understand the difference between what we choose on a soul level and what we experience on a human level. Inhuman treatment such as wartime atrocities, crime, and child abuse, tries our understanding the most. When we look at this on a soul level, it easy to say it is what we chose in order to learn our lessons. However, when we look at this on a human level, within the context of our relationships here on Earth, it is a different story.

What we experience as human to human interaction needs to be addressed as part of our society. The laws we enact against things we consider to be "wrong" need to be viewed in just that way. It is in this context that I comment on how wrong it was to perpetrate the injustices on the native peoples of this continent, just as it is wrong to abuse a child. Recovery from any of these offenses must first be dealt with on a human, emotional level as a separate issue or goal. Only then is it appropriate to take note of the lesson for us as individuals or as a group on a soul level. Therefore, if we look for guidance about our human concerns as well as our soul level lessons in the same place these ancient cultures did, perhaps we will find an answer. I believe the answer is an obvious one: to live in harmony with our environment and with each other, honoring what is sacred within each of us. To this end, I channel the Council and allow them to speak of a plan for personal and planetary transformation.

What amazes me most about the Council of Elders is their consistency and cohesion. It is a complete feeling of oneness where, with other groups, I feel not so tight a bond. With the Council it's as if they have one purpose and one purpose alone—world peace and unity. It is the intensity of this focus that I feel certain adds to the intensity and passion of their energy. With other groups I channel there is a oneness of each being becoming a part of the whole, but with the Council their oneness goes beyond their identity as individuals to encompass their great purpose. In this way, they maintain a tight, specific focus when joined with me.

World peace is often thought of as a political ideal or movement, but I have learned with the Council it comes first as a personal shift. "We teach what we are, and what we are is peace," they lovingly say. Since childhood, it has been my own hope that I could become a part of this global change. Now I see my role in this as being a teacher of peace on a personal level that will, in a very real way, contribute to the overall goal of peace world-wide.

Kari Annan, Secretary General of the United Nations, when interviewed on the *Charlie Rose* show in May of 1997, was heard to say that it is no longer the international boundary disputes, country against country, that disrupts the peaceful state of the world, but the disputes *within* boundaries. So, it comes down to a personal level very quickly. How can we live with each other in peace around the world when we are still bickering among ourselves? And, indeed, doesn't this bickering with our neighbor ultimately come down to how we feel about ourselves? It is cleaning up our backyards that remains the challenge.

Though I have channeled the Council many times, the following piece feels most poignant to me. In it, they describe how the process of personal transformation very quickly translates into a worldview. Read it with an eye toward how you can use your own growth to enhance your family, your community, or the world, keeping in mind that what is most important is not what you do, but who you are.

Red Cloud and the Elders speak:

"Many books about Great Spirit talk about how the world began saying, 'In the beginning there was Creator.' And so it was with my people. We began in our own garden of paradise. We had very humble beginnings. It was not necessary for us to think of ourselves as separate from Creator. We knew we were Creator's children and that because of this, we were creators, too.

"We came from many different places in the heavens, in the stars. We were planted here, not just by Creator but also with the help of the rest of humanity that is spread out in many places in many different galaxies. In this, the planting of the human seed in Earth, we became co-creators with Great Spirit. We are the children of the universe who came to Earth to begin a new experiment: to live in harmony, in peace, and in oneness. We learn as we grow that we are not different and are not separate.

"These teachings are the lessons of the new time, the time of the New Ghost Dance, the Dance of Peace. It is a dance for all of humankind, not just for us. In the past, we asked for the return of our life in the old way, the only way we knew. We also asked for the taking away of the white people. This was not the way of Great Spirit. We have learned much since then in our communion with Creator in our time of peace in the heavens. The sacred places that have held our thoughts in eternal time, the sacred mountains that have held our energies are now merging into this time of yours. We have returned to tell you of these things.

"It is true the time of the sharing of all stories of our peoples has come. It is time to share your stories, too. Tell the tales of your families, of your people, of your own ancestors, and we will listen. There is a time now for the sharing of all these things, a time to honor what is past and what is sacred with all of the tribes of Earth. It is a time to honor the great sacredness within us all. We are all a part of Creator, and in the telling of the sacred tales and stories of all we learn we are not different, but the same.

"Let us not remember any more the fear of the past or the old wounds. Let the anger or hurt not stop us from being one once again. One people, one people of peace. It was not always so, even with our people; we fought over many things. Those times are past, and now we wish to live in peace once more, as it was in the beginning.

"In the history of all peoples there was bloodshed and war. There was fear and pain. Have we not learned that more hatred leads us not into peace but into more fear? All people of Earth must now put down their words of anger and of revenge for what is past. Nothing can change this now. Let us honor what is sacred now and come again to Creator to share all with each other.

"Many of you of the Indian tribes ask, "Why is it that many white people now speak these words; those who know not of our pain and suffering? What do they know of our people?" These are true words. They hold much wisdom. But the wisdom of these words is the past. The wisdom of the New Ghost Dance is to include all and not leave out those who would share peace with us. Many of every tribe now seek peace and seek what is sacred with us. Let us honor all who seek peace and come together in the one light. Who better to ask for peace than those of us who have been hurt most deeply? If we can forgive and move forward, all can.

When the white ones came to the North America, many of us were willing to share all that the Earth was to us. All she had shared with us we knew was meant to be shared with others. We were in Oneness with her and desired to honor her dream of including others in that Oneness also. So let us now continue to move forward in this path, the path of true humans. There is enough to share, enough for all people to live in joy of the true light.

Even though there are now great numbers of people upon the Earth, the Earth still honors us with her abundance. She willingly gives us rain when it is dry, clouds when it is hot, shelter when it is cold, and food when we are hungry. She is able to expand her lands, her entire body to help us have enough. She is wise and wishes to honor us and give to us in this way. Who is wise enough to say no to such a gift. If we receive, we will find peace. Allow all to come to the place of receiving from the Earth. Allow all to honor her desire to care for us. The Earth is abundant in ways you have no wisdom of. She is boundless and knows no limitation. You will see.

I come to you now in peace but also in humility. A humility that speaks not of low self-esteem, but of equality with all beings upon this planet. Do not have pity for yourselves or for us. Pity holds no honor and no sacredness. Pity is the giving of disgrace not the lessening of it. There are no words that take away pain of the past for those who have known hurt. Only forgiveness can do this.

It is now a new time. It is a time where peace is possible once again. In the eternal time that is now, we are the Council. All who desire peace and honor will lead others toward the unity of the one light. The New Ghost Dance of Peace will be done by *all* tribes in *all* nations around the Earth to herald the coming of the New Age, the New Age of Peace for all people. See now how our prayers are answered. We will all dance the dance of the return of the abundance of love on the Earth.

It is only now I am able to come to you in this way to tell you so. You would not have believed this before had I told you. *All people* on the Earth have now come to the place of their own faltering spirits. It is only now that we can all come together in this peace—with open hands, with open hearts and in humility. We all came to the Earth with the same hopes, the same high dreams to build new lives of peace and generosity. In this, we are the same. We come to you knowing it is a time of new beginnings and a time to teach peace to others. In this, we are also the same.

The way to this peace is not through the old way of fear but through the ancient spirit of love. The Earth has this love for us. She is our mother and she will provide for us in ways completely beyond our ability to understand it. It is a love so complete that all people's needs will be answered in loving abundance, fruitful abundance. The Earth has everything we need. We must be humble enough to receive it and wise enough to share it without fear of losing it. It is only then will we all realize that the answer to the sacred prayer of the Ghost Dance is answered.

In the joining of all peoples together without exclusion, the Earth will bless us. It is time to receive the Earth's and Great Spirit's generosity and begin the celebration: the New Ghost Dance of Peace. It is a dance of awakening that will bring all tribes of the Earth together in the sacred peace of Oneness. Then we will all enter into the Oneness *together*. One people, one heart, one purpose, one desire: love."

In subsequent channeling sessions with the Council they have also discussed the concept of how there is only one culture that matters and that is the culture of love, which is the true culture of spirit. They even make reference to not putting their cultures on a pedestal as some New Age devotees do. This is not equality or wholeness; this is exclusion once again. There is no one true Earth culture, they say, that surpasses all others. The one culture is love. Some call it the One Love, or the One Heart.

The inculturation of spirit is ephemeral and gives rise to dogma. The rise of dogma ultimately gives way to the creation of a superstructure of power, ultimately presenting the temptation to abuse that power. We have seen examples of this throughout the ages in all cultures. The only true manifestation of love is love itself. It needs no secondary justification or culture. Becoming that love is the greatest way to represent it. Being love is its own explanation. For that, there is no representation, only an arrow to the truth, a temporary way station for spirit in transition.

The Council illustrates this by saying in a later session:

"There must now be a new plan. That is what the true prayer of the Ghost Dance was. Great Spirit read our hearts so completely, we were given not only the abundance and peace we requested but also a new understanding of our prayer to go beyond what we asked for, to grant us entry into the Oneness of Spirit with all peoples. Only in the new plan is that possible. Only by seeing through culture is this possible. The nature of love cannot be limited to one people's way."

The Council exemplifies true leadership for the world. True leadership is always outside of culture and speaks directly to the individual. In a transcendent way, leadership is a call to the True Self, a call to the genuine and unmistakable part of each person in the world that is loved and embraced for who they are, beyond their personality or their culture. The Council would say, "Let not fear stand in your way of embracing all whom you meet and all who meet you." Go beyond reason to love and become love itself. Embrace all whom desire to embrace you for the sake of love. The Elders often speak of freedom. True freedom is freedom of the spirit: unlimited, unforced, un-dogmatic and unconditional. This is what love is.

Chapter 21

The Dance of Peace

To channel the combined energies of the elders that make up the Council is a little like handling fire. If you do it carefully, without your ego, you will become warmed by their presence. If not, you could get toasted in the process. The warming feeling I get is like sitting snugly in front of a hearth, receiving the goodness of many friends who love me. As in all channeling, trust is a key element.

Channeling the Council it is a little like falling off a cliff and knowing I will be caught but not looking for the hands that will be catching me. This requires lots of faith. So did being a native on various continents that were taken over by an albino-looking people many centuries ago. Faith and trust is what they are all about. If one cannot trust oneself and learn to come to a place of peace within, then connecting with this group of wise leaders is not possible.

Though my first experience with the Council was in a group setting, I had a private session with another couple many months earlier when a "Grandmother," as she called herself, appeared and made herself known to me. She was also a native elder and master in her own right. Her energy was very similar to the Council's, the same strong loving force. It was only in retrospect, long after I had been channeling the Council, that I realized this wise master foretold their coming to me.

I came to know Teri and Steve through doing a psychic fair in one of the outlying areas near my hometown. I had read for Teri at the fair and saw that she had many animal guides that had been with her lifetime after lifetime. She had been a medicine woman in another life and though now a Caucasian, still retained the same loving spirit for the Earth. When I visited Teri and her husband Steve in their home some months after our meeting, they asked me to see if I could connect to the guides for them and bring some information through. I easily agreed.

I got comfortable in a sitting position on their couch and made myself available to my guides. As I "stepped aside" to channel them, my usual group of guides, smaller than it is now, spoke with Teri and Steve for about half an hour. As there was a pause in the information, I felt another presence coming near. As always, I asked this new presence to identify itself. The energy was distinctly feminine and very old. She identified herself simply as "Grandmother." Her energy was strong, loving and peaceful; she was respectful of my free choice, honoring me as an individual and as a "guide" in my own right. She was interested in offering information to Teri through me, and I was happy to assist.

As I allowed her energy to merge with mine, she placed an image of herself in my mind as she appeared in physical form on the Earth many generations ago. As I continued to join with her energy, a picture began materializing of a thin, native woman with glowing, copper-colored skin, gray hair, and a halo of golden light that encircled her entire body. I also saw a majestic owl that hovered close by Grandmother's shoulder. The bird seemed saturated in the purest of wisdom and exuded a pure white light while maintaining a protective, affectionate, and peaceful watch on the elder. There was even a hint of humor in the eyes of the old bird. The light surrounding the woman in my mind seemed to interpenetrate her image and, at the same time, reach out to embrace the couple with whom I was working. It was at this moment she spoke to Teri through me:

"You have endured much hardship in this life, my daughter. Much pain both physical and emotional. You have transcended many difficulties in the physical form transmuting these challenges and rendering them harmless to others because of your faith. You have shown great courage in this and healing has come to many because of your example. Even now, you are destroying old images of fear about the nature of illness and how to release yourself from it. Your spiritual growth has paralleled your physical recovery as well.

"I, too, knew temporal frailties of the body when I was in physical form. As I have transcended all pain now and am in divine alignment, you may come to me often to align your own spirit with mine to find healing and wisdom. Many others have done this, and I will be there for you all. As I once was, I always am.

"Others are with me who offer their services to the many who will come. Each person has their own personal guide who will help them align with the Great Spirit and bring them healing. All that is required is a desire to be healed, and it will be so. Speak to us often, ask for our help and it will be given gladly. It is why we are here. It is why we have come to you now. You and others will need this connection and the comfort that comes with it in the times to come because there will be things happening, changes, that will not be understood by any but the most advanced of you. Others will come after me who will tell you of the details of this." *I feel certain that here, Grandmother foretells of the coming of the Council.* "But for now, have faith. Have faith and persevere. Above all have trust and live strong in your faith.

"I say these things not to bring you to a point of fear, but to prepare you for what is to come and to let you know even now things are not as they appear to be. Cultures and nation-states await decisions by their leaders about what is to come and how this will happen. If your leaders are wise, they will bend like the willow and allow the love that is in their hearts to manifest through them. They will guide their peoples with a strong and courageous hand, lovingly push aside the floodwaters of fear and bring their peoples into a new land of peace. I speak of politics and economics, of course, but other things will change, too. You know of these things, you have all spoken to each other about them. Changes in family structures, in communities, in housing. How all will live in peace together one day…one day. That day has come; it is now.

"Surrender to the light in the same way that the white dove flies up to embrace the sunshine and you will you feel comfort. Know that when the time comes, you will be released from a physical body as I have been. It will not be long in my understanding of time until we are reunited, but do not fear, as you understand it, your time is not yet near. You will transcend your present physical discomforts long before you decide to come to me in spirit without a body. You will flourish in the meantime.

"Transcendence of the physical is here for you as well, the joining with many beings in spirit without the need to leave the body behind. You will all do this. You and many others like you will learn the techniques of this process, and even though it seems impossible for you now, it will come swiftly. Few will be left behind. All that have chosen to do this will come. Learning transcendence will be like learning to walk. It will be difficult at first, frustrating and awkward, but later, with much practice, it will flow smoothly for you, and you will hardly know you are the one doing it. It will simply be like floating along and enjoying the scenery.

"So take heart, feel my presence with you, allow the comfort of my connection with you to flow through your body and you will find healing. You will find health. That is all I have to tell you now. Listen to the others who will come after me, for they, too, will tell you the truth. Not a truth that shifts and changes with winds, as your politicians tell it, but the truth as you desire it. It is the truth of love. Go in peace my daughter."

Though I did not channel "Grandmother" again, I know she is part of the Council of Elders that is with me still. The above text was something

I channeled years before I met the Council, and I am still a bit amazed at how similar their energy and their messages are.

A Native American Elder attended another of my group sessions in which I channeled the Council. I was interested to see how the Council would interact with her since I viewed her as being somehow more "in-tune" with those native energies. I have to admit, when I learned this woman was going to be in attendance that evening I was a little anxious. Would my connection with the Council hold up to her connections that were both spiritual and genetic? Was my wisdom equal to that of hers, or would I make a fool of myself in front of someone who I believed to be something of a cultural icon?

To my surprise, the Council addressed her no differently than anyone else. For me it was the beginning of a level of self-recognition and self-acceptance that would form the foundation of a new-found faith in myself. As our group time began and I allowed my connection with the Council to take shape, I could feel that their love for this woman of their own heritage and experiences was no different than their love for me or for anyone else in the room. It was the last time I would make the mistake of belittling myself by thinking someone held more spiritual power than I did. My learning in this has not only helped me to view myself with more freedom and respect, but I have also been able to work in private sessions with people knowing that regardless of their conscious knowledge of spiritual practices or experiences, we are all equals.

This truth of this was to play out to an even greater extent when, in 2001, I held a workshop that included an audience member who was a well-accomplished Eastern Indian man. I have always admired how the people of India hold fast to their beliefs in the face of unspeakable poverty. Their dedication to their spirituality is profoundly humbling to me. So for me, this man was an icon of a different kind. As the workshop proceeded, I found, a bit to my surprise, that I held information and wisdom this gentle soul did not. Even with years of Yoga and meditation practice, I could still add to his experience. I have learned that we all have things to share from our own soul level wisdom with each other in ways that continues to bring us all closer to oneness.

I have also had time to think about how shallow it was for me to believe that this lifetime of experiences is all that we have to draw upon. In actuality, with lifetime after lifetime of experience, we surely have all played varied roles in different shapes, sexes, colors, and sizes. If I am to believe that this one lifetime alone is all that I am, then I am truly bound in limitation that is not only third-dimensional but also discriminatory. My concept of who we all are in spirit is no longer so limited. Judgment is not just about believing ourselves to be greater or lesser than others, it is about believing that anyone is better than anyone else.

Several weeks after the group with that native elder woman, the following message from the Council came through in another group session. It seems to touch upon just this point. The Council speaks:

"Be most gentle with yourselves. The time of religious beliefs, judgments, and blame is past. You are not here to force yourselves into conforming to some ideological, cultural, or spiritual practices. Do you not know this? Love is the way to life, and loving *yourself* is the first step on this path. Spirit does not judge; this is all you have to understand to heal the old patterns of humankind that did not bear fruit. Once understood, and embraced fully, you will be able to experience something else besides judgment of yourself or others.

"Do not blame yourself if you believe you are not perfect; do not blame or judge others if they are not. What you call sin is simply separation from the knowledge that you are perfect. We did not live in this way. We were one with Creator. So go your way in love and in harmony, and love will envelope you until you can no longer do anything *but* love. Trust and know this will be so.

"Begin to laugh about judgments you make, saying, 'It is good to relax and be one with Creator, I know I am loved.' Love yourself and find joy and goodness in your life here, this is what life is for. As you learn the wisdom of peace, you will see it is a part of the open heart. Judgment is a part of the mind and has no place here. Allow yourself to learn a sense of *feeling* the answers to questions and decisions you must make instead of *thinking* about them. Go to your heart and feel the love *and* knowledge it has to offer you. Your heart is good, and you are a strong being.

"The mind cannot prove wisdom found in the heart. The mind does not feel. When you find wisdom, it feels right, it feels good and gives you peace. This is how we arrive at our wisdom. Feel our words as we offer them to you."

That same evening someone in group had the following question. "Is it significant when a comet appears or other astrological events happen, and how does that affect people's spiritual growth?"

The Council replied, "These are simply messengers that herald the beginning of the new time. Your stories tell that there was a star that heralded the birth of the one of your teachers so long ago? It was a messenger was it not? The movement of the stars foretells all great movements in the Earth. Notice being given, invitations being sent. The birth process that is happening now is being announced to all peoples saying, 'Here is Earth, a place to be recognized. Come, and see for yourself what is happening.'

"It is also a message of the peoples of Earth saying, 'Sit up and take notice about what is happening not only beneath and around you, but most importantly, within you.' What happens in the Earth is also what takes place inside of you. Always the outer, an expression of what happens within. You and Earth mirror each other, each and all in the process of evolution together. This is the oneness we speak of; this is Creator's plan.

"When you see the stars telling you of things to come, receive the love that is sent to you. There is not sign in the sky that does not send love to you. The coming Dance of Peace is a great celebration. Feel this in your hearts and feel glad you are here to take part in it. Many messages of love are being sent to you. Open your hearts to receive this, and take part in the celebration. More love is coming than you have ever seen before. Of all the love you have felt in all your lives, there is more love than this for you. Make yourself ready to dance.

"To prepare yourself, remember who you are. Remember that you are the seed of great beings of love, having come to Earth to unite with each other and with Creator in love and in oneness. See the divine spark you carry, be ready to be this spark. This is what comes for you, to be who you are in divine love and joy, one with Creator. It is time for the great harvest."

The Council concluded the evening with a peaceful benediction that seemed to soothe the hearts and relax the minds of all present.

They said, "Now let us be together in the one love, a time of no aloneness. Feel Earth as she loves you. Not the love of your old world, small and far away, but love as Earth gives, full as the fields of grass, sweet as the flowers, flowing as the spring waters. Let her refresh you as a cool breeze blows on your spirit. Great Spirit knows no distances. There are no spaces that cannot be reached. You are together and you are one in the center of the circle that is love. All beings here love you as we do now. This is the one love we speak of.

"It is just a feeling, a feeling that brings you peace. In the time to come there will be peace between all brothers and sisters. In this inner place of peace, it matters not what fear you still have. Fear cannot keep love away from you. There is no fear that love's gentle hand cannot caress away. Let a feeling of change fill you, a feeling of being in peace with who you are—you, the divine spark. Be at peace now and go into your life in harmony with the knowledge of love that is to come."

Chapter 22

What Lies Beyond

What lies ahead for us all? Where is the love and wisdom we receive from the ascended masters taking us? It is clear that the Earth's problems and challenges cannot be solved by politics and economics alone, or by religion, either. We've all tried these without much success. In order for us to live in peace and balance as a planet, we must first find peace within. To this end, the masters and each of our own spirit guides assist us. Only as the peace within each of us deepens, will it begin to manifest in our daily, local affairs and, hopefully, soon in world affairs.

The world is rapidly becoming a much smaller place, both by exponentially increasing population and increased communication. We are no longer a planet of isolated continents. We are one people, a people of spirit and a people of heart. It is this heartfelt and spiritual connection that draws us closer to one another. When we allow our hearts to begin to speak instead of our intellects or our egos, we find out the truth, which is that we are one. One human people with a great big human heart, a heart that wants to be loved. Isn't this what we all have in common? The desire to know we are loved?

When each of us becomes willing to reach out for that love to a God or a Great Spirit that touches us, we begin to see that we are not different. We share what is common to us all: a desire to live in peace, unencumbered by fear and unobstructed by divisiveness. The greatest example of how we as a planet of different cultures can come together was shown to me years ago during the period in our own history when the fears of cold war were about to begin changing.

I was watching a program on television that was carried by satellite to both the then Soviet Union and the United States. Assembled by the two countries' television networks were groups of each countries' peoples. It seemed both audiences were not chosen for their works of art, their accomplishments in economics, politics or for other notable worldly distinctions. They were the common people from both sides of the globe, and they were all women.

Housewives, mothers, daughters, sisters, they sat in audiences seeing each other on huge television screens. Images that bounced off a bundle of metal and computer chips sitting out in space connected the two worlds. I watched with rapt attention waiting to see what would happen. Would each country criticize the other for repression, propaganda, or for atrocities committed in the name of world domination? Would there be squabbles about military agendas or hunger? What transpired was far from this.

As the assembled women from these two powerful nations convened there was an obvious nervousness within both groups. There was some squirming in chairs and the women though attentive, seemed as uncertain about what would happen. The idea was to give the people of each side a chance to speak to each other without the intervening cacophony of governments and policy makers, a simple human to human contact. It was an awesome moment, a moment in time that seemed to stand still.

I watched as the first woman stood up and was handed a microphone, there was a hush in the two audiences. Translators standing by were also attentive and ready. Though my memory, as in most things, is only partially complete, I recall the gist of what transpired. A woman from the Soviet Union was first to speak. Her question to the waiting women of the United States was this: "Why do you want to make war with us?"

A woman from the U.S. stood up to answer. She replied, "We don't! It is *you* who want to attack us." Perplexed and surprised looks were evident on the faces of the women of both sides. There was a pause as if no one knew where to go from there. A few more questions were asked of an economic and political nature bringing the same looks of frustration, confusion, anger, and fear from the women of both countries.

Then a woman, from which country I do not remember, stood up. She took the microphone in her hand and asked the question that shattered the anxious division of the two groups. Holding the microphone to her mouth she said to a woman standing on other side, "What do you have in your purse?"

It cut to the heart of all present, and I could sense the audiences shift in their seats. As I listened to the response, I felt my eyes glistening with tears. The other woman, a world away, answered without hesitation, "The same as you have in yours, I'm sure." Lipstick, tissues, keys—the things I had in my purse at that moment, too. Suddenly, two women forgetting to be different reached out across the world to each other, across oceans of fear.

A great moment in history occurred when two counties bridged the gap of fear and mistrust. I believe it was no coincidence that this heralded the beginning of the end of the cold war. Coming together—not to find fault or blame, but to see what they had on common—these two women had the courage to reach out to each other and offer the world hope. It was an historic moment that slipped by us while the governments of both countries created more armies and missiles. The power of two women to bridge the gap of fear. I was never the same after that. It was the moment I realized that two people, that one person, could make a difference.

Those two women, are joined by dozens of people, hundreds even thousands around the world, who begin to understand that it's not so important what our governments do or say, what our differences are, or how far apart we may seem. What matters most is what each of us can do to go beyond our fear and reach out to another. This is what the masters are trying to tell us. We *can* make a difference. One person can make a difference.

The masters speak countless times of how we can never understand the "ripple effect" of our actions. They often tell me that when we change on the inside, we change the world. I am reminded of a line in the movie, *Schindler's List,* when Schindler's accountant quotes from the Talmud saying, "He who saves one life, saves the world in time."

Is it arrogance to believe you can make a difference in the world just by changing yourself? I'm certain it isn't. In the readings I have done for people around the world, I have learned many things. Two things stand out for me now. How one person's prayers can and do affect others, and how change for one person on the inside, on a personal level, changes others.

Sometimes the change occurring from either of these things is profound, even astounding. I remember the man in the U.S. who simply, did nothing but pray for his son, and his son's life was turned around. One person. I remember the woman from South Africa who showed up for a reading and ended up blessing me with healing information I was able to share with many, many others. One person. I remember the woman who wanted to know if her friend who had committed suicide, was all right. You have read about them, and of her message of hope from the other side in an earlier passage in this book. One person, asking a simple question.

When you are tempted to think of yourself as only one person, remember the people in your own life who have touched you and helped you. Remember the women in Russia and in the U.S. who reached out to each other across, perhaps what was one of the greatest barriers of fear in their time, to find what they had in common, instead of what was different about them. One person can make a difference. That one person could be you. Use the words in this book to inspire you, to heal you, to touch you and in turn to touch others. Use them to help you simply find a life that is more peaceful, or to become free from worry and fear. Use these words for yourself and make a difference. The world needs more people like you.

There is a community that awaits us all. This community is beyond culture, beyond gender and race, beyond countries and boundaries and beyond fear. It is the community the masters always invite us to enter. It is the community the Council of Elders invite us to become a part of. It is a part of us already because it is within us. It is within our hearts and it is time to come home to this new community. In a way it is a new country, a new and unexplored territory, and we are pioneers in it. It is the community of love, the love that is here for us all. Come home to this place that awaits you with open arms. Meet the others with whom you share this love, this new bond. Come home to love.

Years ago my guides first spoke to me of this saying:

"In the coming years people will be joining together and bonding with each other in order to prepare for the changes to come and move more fluidly into the energy of the New Earth. Those who have already begun this process of inner learning have started sharing all they are and all they have with others in the spirit of love. Even seeming strangers—though not strangers of the heart!—offer assistance to those who are also heart-centered. This brings about change more smoothly. Many changes that are to come will, in themselves, create the need for people bonding together. The need for small villages and small communities grouping together to aid one another will become the cornerstone of new societies.

"Large governing bodies around the world that believe themselves to be fully in their power will feel themselves losing power over individuals. Many governmental officials already know this. Many people in the private sector with economic powers that affect and sway governments already know this as well. This is not something to be feared. Imagine, the old systems that used to keep you locked into a fear-based, rigid and ruthless pattern, draining your energies both financial and emotional will no longer prevail. You are free to express who you are in your hearts without anyone telling you that you will be taxed for it!

"Can you begin to catch a glimpse of the essence of what is to come? The free exchange of goods and services founded on a heart-based loving connection with one another, small communities, sharing their work, their lives, their needs, their hopes and dreams. Following those dreams right up into a new way of living where co-creation with the Divine is not a distant ideology of an age to come, but the loving medium of the fabric of your new lives, an altered time and space where love prevails. It is true. It is coming. Believe it and prepare to be enveloped in love."

Appendix A
Meet the Masters

As Djwal Khul says: "To connect with the essence of a particular master, you must be open to the *flow* of love instead of being open to a fixed or specific being with a name. You must float with this and allow your essence to co-mingle with theirs. It is a different feeling than that of being alone in your body. It is not strictly a third-dimensional experience; it is yet intangible for you. Since you are moving into the realm of many intangibles there will be a range of senses to which you will gradually become acclimated. Simply be open to *all* experiences without judgment and without expectation. Then you will be ready to learn many new things."

Here are the masters of the preceding pages. I have listed a couple of them whose channeled messages I did not have quite enough space to incorporate into this book. All the same, enjoy a connection with all of them in your own meditation or walks in nature.

Archangel Gabriel: I include this being in my list to show you how unlimited joy can be. I do not offer one of his channelings, but if I did, it would probably be filled with so much laughter it would be hard to transcribe. The only way possible to describe what my experience with channeling this one is to say I felt like I had my body and spirit filled with champagne. When Gabriel is with me, I feel filled with bubbles and joy to the point of being positively effervescent! Imagine someone pouring Alka-seltzer into your spirit, so much bubbly energy it is hard to contain.

In my few experiences with channeling Gabriel in groups, I have seen almost the entire audience laugh, too. Those who weren't laughing were such tough characters, I don't think anything could have lightened them up. White is unmistakably his color, the kind of white that is like the clouds.

Archangel Michael: Guardian and protector of the innocent. One thing is for sure about Michael; he is very big. Often when I have channeled him, I feel as if I am seven or eight feet tall! My friends have said this is how he/I appear to them when they are watching me channel.

His presence in me has made me feel like I have a spine of steel and at the same time there is a hint of laughter. Perhaps this because he knows just how invincible he is. His presence is hard to mistake for the other masters because of the sheer authority of it. He can be gentle, and often is, but his energy is not small by any means.

The color I often associate with Michael is a clear looking almost opaque white that is distinctly not of this world. The strongest indication I have of Michael's arrival is the knowledge that he knows he is more powerful than anything in this realm. It is his job to be strong, and he does it well. Do not mistake this with aggressiveness, though. It could not be further from the truth. Michael will laugh with you and enjoying the flow of ease and comfort while still being the tallest being in the room.

Djwal Khul: He is one of my favorite beings to channel for the sheer pleasure of it. Always eager to teach, play and heal, this master, famous for his earlier work with Alice Bailey, cajoles, inspires and lifts the hearts of those with whom he speaks. D.K., as I call him, is an earthy healer that excels in herbology, natural healing, and communication with the plant and animal kingdoms. His energy is light, his colors are green and sparkling bronze, and he knows much about how to live a balanced life.

If you want to learn how to live with ease and comfort, consult D.K. He will show you the uselessness of worry, the futility of fear, and lead you to a new way of being. His down-to-earth approach is disarming, and in speaking to him, it is often hard to remember why you were ever worried to begin with. "Life is simple," he says, "let it be."

El Morya: The warrior, the lover, the master of conquest, these and other such names befit this strong master. I don't channel him frequently, but when I do, he often rivals Archangel Michael for intensity. His presence cannot be missed. His color is without question, red and with all the passion red embodies. A former warrior in battle while on Earth, he has now assumed a more gentle, yet no less powerful, position of teacher and guide.

El Morya is passionate, earthy and sensual, his laugh is liquid. His passion is unbridled when he is helping others to see the Divine. He is unequivocal when teaching, almost demanding that passion be brought to fullness by divine connection. Otherwise, it is impotent. For any of you who have read about and felt connection with El Morya, you will know his passion while on Earth was a great aspect of his physical being. His passion is no less diminished in spirit only transformed and fulfilled, completed by union with God.

Kuthumi: A master from Kashmir, it is said, a self-actualized being who not that long ago walked the earth as a spiritual teacher in India and the surrounding area. He has been given the title *World Teacher*. His energy feels gentle yet strong and sustaining. His keen mind is able to penetrate even the deepest confusion with a superlative ability to explain even the most difficult and challenging spiritual questions as if they were a child's ABCs. He never has made me feel foolish for asking even the most basic questions.

Kuthumi often seems to be surrounded and interpenetrated with a bluish/turquoise and white light. His presence, though not heavy and physical, has a substance that others seem to lack. His solid "feel" in spirit often brings the assurance that the guidance he is about to render will be weighty and solid, too. His master intelligence, though, is not to be confused with the intellect. He will often come into your mind but not in a way that guides you to use your brain. It is rather his way of validating your own knowledge, while softly shifting you from intellect to heart and spirit.

Kwan Yin: This master is one who loves to heal both physical and emotional wounds. Her invitation to engage the spirit realm and join her in the etheric is most compelling. I have often watched clients follow her gentle lead right into their own hearts and away from control and fear. She is non-threatening, wise, determined, and persistent. These are the tools I have seen her use to heal.

Her energy is a green of many shades, especially a new green like that of spring but not quite of Earth. It has an illusive quality all its own that defies description. Perhaps because it is not truly of the physical realm. I have often seen traces of gold interspersed with her energy but again a feeling of being out of Earth's ken always accompanies her. Mystical, illusive, gentle and strong, these are the qualities I have always associated with Kwan Yin. Ask her for healing and she will be as clear as the rain, as persistent as the sun, and as gentle as a doe. (Her name is sometimes spelled Quan Yin.)

Mother Mary: What is there to say about this divine being of pure love? So infinitely gentle is she that I have never seen anyone be able to resist her open arms. She holds a place in her heart for each of us. Her purity is unmistakable, her gentleness and love are unstoppable. Uniquely able to cross the veil at will, she will often manifest in physical form as she has done in many places around the world.

Once during a time of stress, I was lying face down on my bed contemplating my current difficulties and I felt a hand on my back. I could feel pressure, heat and comfort flowing from it. I could feel it so strongly that even though I knew I was alone in the room, I was compelled to turn around and see if someone was there. I was alone, of course, but I knew Mary had paid me a visit.

A being of such intensity, her influence extends far beyond Earth and her origins are as vast. She often reveals herself in the midst of a blue/white light or at times simply pure white or pink. She has also manifested to me as a brilliant golden peach color. Her waves of warmth and reassurance often precede her. A deep and abiding sense of peace is her hallmark.

Red Cloud, Moccasin, and the Council of Elders: Of all the guides and masters I have channeled, these are the most profound. The Elders are a group of ascended masters that represent most of the indigenous tribes of Earth. Their power is astounding to me. It far surpasses anything I have yet to encounter in the higher dimensions. The first time I channeled the Elders, Moccasin spoke. She is a guide known only to me (that I know of) and speaks simply and clearly for the group.

The power of these masters' energy is so forceful that my first experience channeling them had me holding onto the edges of my chair lest I be lifted right off of it! My body felt transformed into a rocket that was about to take off. For this reason, I am certain they speak to me from way beyond the fifth dimension.

Saint Germain: There is one word I cannot help associating with this being and though it is an earthly, perhaps human quality, still it persists in my mind; that word is sardonic. I always feel that he has a slight smile on his face when I channel him. Like a court jester, he will trick you out of your intellect and bring you into your heart in an often humorous, if roundabout, way. I know other channels to whom Germain is strong, even strict or severe, but I have never seen or felt him this way.

His energy feels like warm water, surrounding me with peace and connection without any rough edges. His ever-present sense of laughter at the foibles of us humans is what I enjoy most about him. He was human in his time, of course, in France actually, and while he is laughing at us, I know he is also laughing at himself, too. I don't usually associate a color with Germain but if I had to, I could say his energy is more blue than red or yellow. He is said to have lived as Merlin, though, I have never asked him if this is true. It is enough for me to know him as the one who talks people right out of their minds.

Sananda: Jesus, as he was known when he was here in human form, is perhaps the master whose earthly life we all know the most about. Even so, I have come to know him not as the "Son of God" but as a part of what God is, what we all are. This is the understanding he has given me, that we are all equal and that together we make up what is "God." Ever humble, always as loving as Mary, I associate Sananda with a youthful glow. A white and golden light seems to emanate from him and though this, too, is another earthly epithet, I would say he is often happy. Perhaps joyful is more correct, but I know he delights to see us wanting his help and being open enough to receive it.

His energy is felt at first loving and then scholarly. His wisdom, unmatched even by Kuthumi, is seen in his ability to boil down lengthy or deep subjects to simple yet profound images and thoughts. His mastery in including everyone in his love and teaching marvels me. He has often compared himself to us here, making himself infinitely approachable. He loves to touch people physically, and when I channel him, I am often compelled to lay a hand on a shoulder or touch a hand in comfort.

So these are my friends or at least a few of them. Enjoy their messages and their personalities in the proceeding chapters. Know that they are as eager to speak with you as they have always been with me and the others for whom I have channeled them. Undoubtedly, you will come to know many things about them I do not. You will forge your own relationships with them as with your own spirit guides and angels. Though I have been doing this for many years, what is most important for you is your own experience. Nothing can replace that. Talk with the masters and see what they have to tell you, open your own heart and receive the blessings they wish to shower upon you. Trust yourself and trust what you hear. And remember most of all: You are not alone.

Appendix B
Simple Guide to Meditation

Previously published in Inner Realm and Open Minds.

The people I work with often ask me to teach them how to meditate. In Zen, it is said the person most receptive in meditation is the novice. This is because the novice has no expectations and therefore is likely to remain open to anything he or she will experience. In looking at how to meditate, this is a good place to start.

Meditation could be called the openness to experience what the five senses cannot detect. My clients often comment that they have a hard time meditating because they cannot block out all thoughts and feelings. Actually, I don't recommend this anyway. In my own meditation, I have often experienced ideas coming to my mind and sensing emotions just below the surface that were exceedingly helpful to me. Meditation then is not trying to block out all experience, it is being prepared for a heightened sense of awareness that leads us to the realm of spirit.

Let's begin with a few key concepts. I call them the four cornerstones of meditation. Relax, let go, allow, and receive. In our everyday world, quiet time is often at a premium. Between jobs, family, commuting, and other tasks, a few minutes of alone time is often a precious commodity.

Why not look at spending a few minutes just relaxing? When we relax and take time to bring in a few deep breaths, often the body's physiology is changed creating receptivity to peace and healing.

Relaxation can take many forms. For people not used to "sitting" in meditation in the traditional sense, I suggest a walk in nature or sitting in your garden. A walk is helpful because it gives you something to do while your mind is benefiting from the relaxation. As you walk, breathe deeply and notice the smell of the air, trees, and flowers, and sounds you are unaccustomed to hearing. Allow your whole body to become the observer. This is a good way of taking your focus off your intellect.

Next, as you bring in the sounds, sights, and smells of nature, gradually let go of whatever your mind wants to focus upon. If worries or problems keep coming to mind, acknowledge these thoughts but breathe, relax and refocus your other senses on smells, the rhythm of your breathing, sounds, and sensations just below the range of your normal observations. Each time your mind wants to interrupt your relaxation, breathe, let go, and relax. There will be plenty of time after your walk to worry, fret, and rehash your fears. Even now these things seem silly don't they?

The next step is perhaps the most important, allow. Allowing is a lot like finding acceptance—acceptance of the things we cannot control, change, or affect, acceptance of our fears and frailties. It is at this point that many people give up. They hit a wall of frustration, feel defeated. They throw in the towel because they can't make their meditation happen. By very definition, this step is not about "making it happen." This is where we really let go of control. It is also the place of faith, the faith that there are other beings, energies, spirit guides, and God itself, helping us to do what we cannot do ourselves. Allowing is like breathing in the smells of nature. We cannot create the smells, but we can benefit from them. It is a subtle shift, a very delicate balance between acting and sensing.

In allowing, you accept all things in your life as they are right now without trying to change them or predict how they will turn out. This way, if there is a simple piece of guidance or a few words of wisdom you are open to hearing them instead of being the one to create it. Allowing is the preparation to receiving. If you do these steps and still feel frustrated try *feeling* the frustration on an emotional level and really let it rip! Give yourself over to it and feel it to the core. Frustration is an emotion just like any of the others and usually when we let ourselves feel it, it shifts itself often revealing other emotions beneath it. This is a productive way of deepening your meditation, too.

Our final step, receiving, is actually very similar to what I call "doing nothing." When *you* do nothing, it allows the world of spirit to *do* the giving. This is the place of receiving the guidance, healing and peace you desire—the abundant rewards of meditation. By letting in guidance, feelings, and suggestions that don't come from your intellect, you often arrive at solutions to situations that you could never before have imagined. The human being has unfathomable depths upon which to draw. Only when we let go of trying to figure everything out with our minds can we truly plumb these depths.

As you begin receiving, pay particular attention to what you feel because the emotions play a key role in healing the mind and body. As you connect with the subtle level of feelings and awareness in your spirit, relax even deeper and receive more. The more you practice this, the easier it will get. Take time to reflect gently on what you wish to heal within yourself or upon what guidance you wish to receive. Allow yourself to become aware of it without trying to solve it with your mind. Receive whatever feelings or thoughts come. When your emotions are stirred do not push them away, feel them and receive guidance. By healing the emotions, you heal the body.

Meditation can be a successful tool for decreasing stress, creating deep relaxation, and even for receiving the guidance that will allow you to live a more balanced, abundant, and peaceful life. Whether you take a walk in nature or simply sit quietly with a cup of tea in your kitchen, your mind, body, and heart will benefit immensely. Enjoy the flow!

ABOUT THE AUTHOR

Carol Sydney is a psychic, channel and teacher who works with people around the world helping them to bridge the gap between the physical and spiritual worlds. She is a contributor to *Sedona Journal of Emergence*, *Die Boschaften* (Germany), and other periodicals nationally and internationally. In addition to channeled articles, she also writes on topics such as meditation, healing, spirit guides and others. She travels around the world holding channeling sessions, doing private readings, and teaching.

With a Bachelor's Degree in Psychology Carol's background includes: counseling, Twelve-Step Outward Bound counseling, adolescent intervention programs, and personal empowerment training. In addition, she teaches channeling, meditation, spirit guide connection, and other metaphysical subjects. Look for her next book, *The New Ghost Dance* to be released in 2002.

When not on tour channeling or teaching, Carol can be found at her home in Sedona, Arizona enjoying the magic of the desert and the abundance of life that flourishes there.

To contact Carol for a personal appointment or to schedule a workshop:

Carol Sydney
P.O. Box 20594
Sedona, AZ 86341

928-284-5373
sedonamagic@earthlink.net

Or you can visit Carol's Web site at: www.carolsydney.com

Made in the USA
Middletown, DE
13 January 2015